Flipping the Format on the Fear of Failure

Licensed2BBadass: A Roadmap for Radio Professionals on Overcoming Fear, Building Resilience, and Thriving in the Industry

Kelly Orchard, Licensed Psychotherapist.

With contributions by Mike McVay, McVay Media Consulting.

Contents

INTRODUCTION

Why We Must Flip the Format on Fear

W.K.R.P. Framework Alignment: Full-Spectrum Preview

Winning Mindset — Know Thyself — Resilience & Responsibility — Positive Psychology

Welcome to the Revolution

This is not your typical radio book. And that's the point.

You've probably read books about management, talent coaching, programming, and sales. You've seen the endless headlines about radio dying, podcasting taking over, and how to make your station go viral on TikTok. But what if I told you the biggest disruption in radio isn't technology, revenue models, or platforms?

It's fear.

Fear of failure. Fear of irrelevance. Fear of burnout, being replaced, or not being good enough. That fear shows up everywhere: in leadership meetings, in programming decisions, in how we treat talent, and in how we talk to ourselves.

This book is about flipping the format on that fear.

What Are You Afraid Of?

We don't always recognize fear when it shows up. It wears disguises—like procrastination, perfectionism, avoidance, or

1

overworking. It convinces us that the safe route is the smart route. That if we just do what we've always done, maybe no one will notice how uncertain we feel.

But fear is sneaky. It hijacks potential. It shrinks creativity. And if we're not careful, it becomes the default setting.

When you operate from fear, you're not leading—you're managing crisis.

What are you afraid of? That you're not good enough? That you'll be found out? That someone younger, faster, or more tech-savvy will take your place?

It's time to flip the format.

How We Got Here

Radio is an industry built on resilience and reinvention. We've gone from vinyl to digital, carts to clouds, and towers to streams. But while the tech evolved, our emotional and leadership frameworks didn't always keep up.

I grew up in radio. My father was a broadcast engineer who taught me the ropes while I was still in pigtails. By the time I was a teenager, I was splicing reel-to-reel tape, scheduling traffic logs, and sweeping the studio floor. Later, I worked in sales, programming, promotions, consulting, and compliance.

I lived it all. And I broke down from it, too.

A health crisis forced me to reevaluate everything. It ended one career—and launched another. I became a psychotherapist, and eventually a leadership coach for professionals in broadcasting and beyond. What I saw in the counseling room and the control room was the same:

People are exhausted. Leaders are overwhelmed. And talent is terrified.

So I decided to build a bridge between what I knew from radio and what I know now from psychology. That's how *Licensed2BBadass* was born. And that's how this book came to be.

What It Means to Flip the Format

In radio, flipping the format means you're radically changing what goes over the air. You change the music, the imaging, the vibe — and usually, you do it with one big stunt to get attention.

This book is your stunt.

But instead of flipping your playlist, we're flipping your mindset. We're updating the inner software that drives your leadership, creativity, and culture. We're going to deprogram the fear-based conditioning and install something more powerful: purpose, clarity, confidence, and connection.

The W.K.R.P. Framework in this book will help you do that.

The W.K.R.P. Framework: Your New Leadership Signal

Each section of this book aligns with one pillar of this evidence-based approach:

- **W: Winning Mindset** — We start with mental fitness. You'll learn how to overcome fear of failure and build a mindset that thrives in uncertainty.

- **K: Know Thyself** — We dive into identity, values, and emotional intelligence. Because you can't lead others well until you understand yourself.

- **R: Resilience, Responsibility & Respect** — We explore how to bounce back from setbacks, take ownership, and create trust-based cultures.

- **P: Positive Psychology** — We finish by anchoring in what works. Science-backed strategies for thriving teams, confident communication, and sustainable leadership.

Victorville: Where the Lessons Got Real

Before radio consolidation, before therapy, before I was a published author, there was Victorville. A high desert town. A small FM station. A family operation with duct-taped equipment and big dreams.

That's where I learned the basics—and the breakthroughs.

Like how one strategic stunt (looping "Papa Was a Rolling Stone") generated more buzz than a full marketing budget. Or how a DJ's offhand comment spiraled into city-wide panic. Or how one programmer mentored me not with praise, but with trust.

These aren't polished stories. They're real ones. And they taught me that leadership isn't about having all the answers. It's about staying grounded, open, and willing to flip your own internal format when it stops working.

This Isn't a Pep Talk. It's a Pattern Disruptor.

I won't tell you to hustle harder, lean in, or manifest success through mantras. I'll show you how fear works in your brain, how to outsmart your inner critic, and how to apply proven leadership strategies that actually work in media.

There will be tools. There will be worksheets. There will be some loving, evidence-based butt-kicking.

What You'll Get from This Book:

- How to recognize fear-based leadership—and replace it with confident clarity
- Ways to coach yourself and others with curiosity instead of control
- Real stories from inside radio that will make you laugh, cry, and think
- Science-backed tools for managing mindset, energy, conflict, and creativity
- A new definition of leadership that actually fits our industry

You don't have to fake confidence anymore. You don't have to hide your struggle. You don't have to run on adrenaline and hope it gets easier.

You just need to flip the format.

So turn the page. Cue the mic. Let's rewrite what leadership sounds like in this business.

Let's flip the format on fear.

PART 1

W — Winning Mindset

Chapters 1–3

CHAPTER 1

Why Fear Is Running the Show (And How to Flip It)

W.K.R.P. Framework: Winning Mindset
Fear in the Radio Industry: The Silent Saboteur

Fear is the biggest thief of opportunity. It doesn't just steal confidence—it cripples action. It stops professionals from taking risks, speaking up, making bold moves, and trusting their instincts. And in the radio industry, fear often runs the show.

📻 A market manager fears losing advertisers, so they resist format changes—until ratings plummet.

📻 An on-air personality fears negative listener feedback, so they play it safe—and lose their audience.

📻 A station owner fears shifting to digital, so they ignore industry trends—until their station becomes irrelevant.

Fear is behind stagnation, poor decision-making, and career burnout. But here's the good news: fear is just a mental program—and it can be reprogrammed.

Personal Story: The Day I Had to Face Fear Head-On

I know fear. I've lived it. It came for me in the middle of my career, when everything was going great. I was 42 years old and thriving in the radio industry. I had built a career consulting, managing stations, and leading teams. Then, out of nowhere, I was diagnosed with congestive heart failure.

📌 Would I ever work again?

📌 Would I become irrelevant?

📌 Had I peaked?

Fear whispered that my career was over. But fear was wrong. Instead of letting it control me, I decided to flip the format on fear itself. I pivoted into coaching, leadership development, and psychology — blending my radio experience with mental resilience strategies. I embraced uncertainty, choosing to see it as an open door, not a dead end. I reprogrammed my mindset, understanding that fear is just a signal, not a stop sign. That shift in mindset — not my credentials, not my experience — was what transformed my future.

From Fear to Influence: Lessons from the Back Office

When I was younger, I thought that to be influential, I needed a powerful title or a high-profile role. But my journey in the radio industry taught me something very different. My role began in the back office. I did traffic and billing, recorded and scheduled public service announcements, ran errands, swept floors, and even handled janitorial duties. I wasn't handed influence — I created it through commitment and consistency.

In my article "How to Be Influential in Any Role," I explained that influence is built when you understand how your presence and performance shape your environment. I learned that doing the small things right, over and over again, builds credibility. And when people trust your work, they begin to value your voice.

Leadership doesn't begin with a promotion. It begins with stepping up, being seen, and being dependable. When fear tells you, "You're not ready," action is the antidote. Show up. Lean in. That's how you influence change from any seat in the house.

Insider Insight: Mike McVay on Leadership Under Pressure

Fear is whatever we make it. One of the luckiest moments in my life was when I was given the opportunity to be Program Director at a Los Angeles Top-40 station at the young age of 24. That's something that probably wouldn't happen today.

I arrived at KTNQ (10Q) in Los Angeles from Charleston, WV. The airstaff included Charlie Tuna, Jack Armstrong, The Real Don Steele, Machine Gun Kelly, and Nancy Plum. Highly successful, well-known talent, all of whom had much greater experience than me. Coaching them seemed surreal and it was frightening. My approach was to admit my shortcomings given my lack of experience. I asked each talent about their shows, what they liked and disliked about them, and I asked how they liked to be coached. They responded well to that approach.

My growth as a Program Director and Talent Coach took a giant step forward because I learned from them. Once when speaking publicly, I was asked a question about talent I worked with and admired. My response began by saying "Some of the best air talent I've ever worked for …" I didn't realize I'd answered with those words until someone pointed it out to me. Working FOR the talent was my way of enabling us and the station to accomplish our goals.

The Science of Fear: Why We Freeze Instead of Act

Fear isn't logical—it's biological. It's the brain's ancient survival mechanism, designed to protect us from threats. But in modern life, our brains can't tell the difference between a real danger (like a bear chasing us) and a perceived one (like pitching a new show or making a career pivot).

◯ The Amygdala Hijack – When we feel fear, our brain triggers fight, flight, or freeze—stopping logical decision-making.

◯ Fear Strengthens Neural Pathways – The more we give in to fear, the stronger those fear-based circuits become.

◯ Fear Blocks Creativity & Risk-Taking – It keeps us small, safe, and stuck.

But here's the game-changer: the brain is neuroplastic. With effort and awareness, we can train our minds to react differently to fear. That starts with understanding where our fear originates—and taking action to challenge it.

Victorville Blog Story: It's Only Victorville

Even with the best laid plans we encounter obstacles. I recently suffered some personal and professional setbacks. Although I don't post each and every detail for the world to see (take my advice, not everyone needs to know the nitty gritty details of your life), I'm happy to share what I've learned.

An article was written about me and published in the Victorville newspaper, and I received numerous phone calls and messages on my social networks "congratulating" me. I'm not certain what the "congrats" were for, the story merely shared what I've been up to since I left the airwaves in Victorville – but it was a really nice piece (a few inaccuracies, but that can be expected and forgiven).

On the very same day, I experienced a professional setback that will delay my forward moving progress for a while. Of course, like anyone else – I was disappointed, discouraged and frustrated at what my immediate automatic response was, "I'm NEVER going to achieve what I've been working so hard for."

Have you been experiencing setbacks too? I'd venture to say that we all are right now.

I wanted to say to myself, …It's Only Victorville, but had to laugh, because that would be insulting to the fact that the Victorville newspaper just published an article about me, and I received some fabulous response from it! Go figure!

It's the setback that has me saying, "…It's Only Victorville".

I can and will move forward. Here's how I managed to work through it:

- I listened to my professional colleagues who gave me sound insight and encouragement not to beat myself up over it.

- I allowed my family to provide me with consolation, knowing how hard I've been working – while still managing to take care of some immediate family crises.

- I processed it in a way that was healthy for my mind, body and spirit.

- I had a heart-to-heart chat with my Dad… who without hesitation, shared some stories of his own professional setbacks, and once again reminded me that it's not the end of the world.

Disappointments, obstacles, setbacks and failures are all part of the growth process. Never give up on something that is really important to you – especially if you've been working so hard at it.

When I speak to people about it, it's important to know the difference between letting go of something that wasn't meant to be, or hanging on because it wasn't meant to be, right now.

That's where I send you back to following your heart, your instincts and intuition.

Life can change so quickly, so here are a few quick tips:

- Breathe in, and be present in the moment, because it won't stay that way forever!
- Do a positive activity to counter the negative one.
- Talk to a trusted friend or family member.
- Have a good cry, but don't wallow in self pity.
- Re-focus, recharge and re-strategize. You can DO this!
- Give yourself permission to "grieve" that loss.
- Dare to dream a new dream if necessary.
- Eat healthy, drink water, get out in the fresh air – it really helps!
- Be willing to change your perspective on the circumstances.
- Don't blame others or rationalize too much.
- Don't analyze too much. Too much analysis causes paralysis!
- Practice gratitude for the lessons you've learned and what you DO have.

Educational Insight: Leadership Theory and Locus of Control

In graduate school, I explored multiple models of leadership and intelligence. One of the key frameworks that stuck with me came from a study on leadership effectiveness and functional intelligence. According to the theory, leadership is not about holding a position of power. It is a dynamic social process—a collaboration between leaders and followers guided by shared goals.

The model highlights three essential behaviors for leaders:

- Image Management (appearing competent and trustworthy),

- Relationship Development (understanding follower needs), and

- Resource Deployment (strategically using individual and team strengths).

What resonated with me most was the concept of locus of control. This theory helped me understand that effective leaders operate from an internal locus—they believe they have control over their outcomes. This belief leads to higher motivation, resilience, and clarity. When I realized I could define my path, rather than wait for approval, I became the leader I was always meant to be.

This insight shaped my leadership identity: democratic, team-oriented, and ethically grounded. As I shared in my personal reflection from grad school, my values are deeply influenced by my upbringing, faith, and the real-world lessons of building a radio station with my family. Education didn't create my leadership style—it gave language and validation to what I already knew through experience.

Apple a Day: Say No to Fear

Let's say "no" to fear. What do you fear the most? Fear of rejection? Fear of success? Poverty, homelessness, failure? Fear is False Evidence Appearing Real. In his inaugural address, President Franklin D. Roosevelt said, "We have nothing to fear but fear itself."

The Bible offers a beautiful message on fear, found in Luke chapter 12, verses 22 through 24: "…Do not be anxious about your life, what you will eat, nor about your body, what you will put on. For life is more than food, and the body more than clothing. Consider the ravens: they neither sow nor reap, they have neither storehouse nor barn, and yet God feeds them. Of how much more value are you than the birds!"

How do you overcome and say no to fear? Embrace it. Challenge it. Seek that which you fear most and you will overcome it!

"Everything you want is on the other side of fear." - Jack Canfield

Move yourself into a season of positive growth by just saying no to fear!

Flipping the Format on Fear: The W.K.R.P. Winning Mindset Shift

Fear isn't reality—it's a prediction. And predictions can be wrong. To win in radio (and in life), we must flip the format on fear.

🚀 Instead of thinking, "What if I fail?" → Ask, "What if I succeed?"

🚀 Instead of avoiding challenges → See them as opportunities.

🚀 Instead of dwelling on past failures → Focus on future growth.

The winning mindset means choosing courage over comfort. It means seeing fear not as an obstacle, but as a signal to grow.

Actionable Worksheet: Rewriting Your Fear Script
Step 1: Identify Your Top 3 Career Fears

What are the biggest fears holding you back in your radio career? Write them down.

Step 2: Examine the Worst-Case Scenario

For each fear, write out the worst possible outcome. Then, write out what you would do if that happened. Often, you'll discover the fear is survivable.

Step 3: Flip the Format

Rewrite each fear with a positive alternative thought.

Example:

✗ "I'm afraid my station will be outdated." → ✅ "My experience makes me uniquely equipped to evolve with the industry."

Step 4: Take One Small, Brave Action

Choose one small action to challenge your fear today.

Final Thoughts: Fear is a Choice

Fear will always be there, whispering doubts and worst-case scenarios. But you decide how much power it holds over you. You're already a professional, a creator, a leader. You're already doing badass things.

Now it's time to own it.

🚀 You've been licensed to be BadAss—whether anyone gave you that title or not.

Next Up: The Science Behind Fear and Failure

In Chapter 2, we'll dive deeper into how the brain processes fear, and how we can rewire it to work in our favor—not against us.

CHAPTER 2

Understanding the Science of Fear and Failure

W.K.R.P. Framework: Winning Mindset

Fear Is a Mental Program — But You Can Rewrite It

Fear doesn't just paralyze action — it distorts reality. It makes opportunities look like risks and challenges feel impossible. But fear is not fact; it's a prediction. The good news? Predictions can be updated. And because fear is a biological process, not a permanent flaw, we can learn how to work with it instead of being ruled by it.

The Brain on Fear: Why We Freeze Instead of Act

Fear isn't just emotional — it's neurological. It begins in the amygdala, the brain's fear center, which interprets threats and triggers our survival responses: fight, flight, or freeze.

In the radio world, fear often hijacks logic:

- A program director resists change because the brain equates a new format with professional risk.

- A host avoids pitching an idea because rejection triggers a threat response.

- An engineer hesitates to speak up about outdated equipment, fearing they'll be blamed if something fails.

When the amygdala takes over, our prefrontal cortex (responsible for logic, reasoning, and creativity) shuts down. This is called the Amygdala Hijack. It's why we freeze or self-sabotage instead of stepping forward. But here's where neuroscience gives us hope: the brain is neuroplastic. We can change the way we think, feel, and act.

How Fear Manifests in Radio Professionals

In my work with radio stations, I've seen fear take many forms:

- Fear of losing relevance in a rapidly changing media landscape.
- Fear of being replaced by AI or younger talent.
- Fear of financial instability due to industry shifts.
- Fear of failure when trying something new.
- Fear of judgment when voicing a bold opinion.

These fears don't just stay in your head. They show up as procrastination, burnout, perfectionism, creative paralysis, or avoiding leadership roles. One of the most eye-opening insights I learned from reviewing research (and living it!) is this:

"Failing makes you worry that people will lose interest in you... that you're not smart enough... that you're disappointing people. So, you lower expectations or distract yourself with busywork. You may even self-sabotage unconsciously."

In other words: fear lives in our patterns. And those patterns are programmable — just like a format.

The Real Cost of Fear-Based Thinking

Fear-based thinking costs more than confidence. It costs companies billions in lost productivity, turnover, and burnout. It costs individuals their health, joy, and potential.

When fear dominates our thoughts, it leads to:

- Negative thought loops that reinforce anxiety
- Diminished creativity
- Risk aversion and stagnation
- Shallow relationships built on safety, not trust
- Missed opportunities for growth

But here's the kicker: most fear responses operate unconsciously. You might believe you're just being "realistic" when you're actually operating out of outdated fear wiring.

Apple A Day - Say No to Fear

This insight hit me one morning when I was sitting with a client who couldn't take the next step in their career because they were too afraid of failing in public. I handed them this very message — and now I'm handing it to you.

Say no to fear. That's it. You've been saying yes to fear for far too long. Yes, to second-guessing yourself. Yes, to staying silent when you wanted to speak. Yes, to procrastination and perfectionism and waiting for permission.

It's time to say no.

No to worrying about what they think.

No to playing it safe just to avoid criticism.

No to shrinking when you should speak up.

Say no to fear—and yes to courage, curiosity, and badassery. Move yourself into a season of positive growth by just saying no to fear.

Risk Aversion Is Killing Radio

I was asked once to write an article about "fear in radio." It's a common subject among my clients as a Licensed Psychotherapist who also happens to be a radio veteran. When I conduct "Badass Certification" workshops, one of the things we address is FEAR.

There is a lot of fear in radio right now. Fear of change. Fear of losing our jobs. Fear of losing listeners. Fear of trying new things. Fear of letting go of what used to work in the past.

This fear is what leads to *risk aversion*—a refusal to experiment or grow.

Instead, we stay in our comfort zone and call it safe. But safety doesn't lead to innovation. It doesn't build excitement. It doesn't inspire talent or attract new listeners. It doesn't retain the passionate professionals we need to thrive.

When fear wins, radio loses.

I'm a second-generation broadcaster. I grew up in radio. I know what it was like when creativity was valued, when taking a risk meant you might stumble—but you might also break new ground. That's what we did. We broke rules. We tried new formats. We launched bold promotions. We said YES to wild ideas because we were excited about the *possibility* of winning.

Now, too many stations are stuck in survival mode. Upper management is fearful of legal issues, PR disasters, losing revenue, offending someone, or looking bad. And that fear trickles down. Programmers stop innovating. On-air personalities are afraid to speak freely. Promotions are safe, boring, predictable.

Risk aversion is a creativity killer.

In therapy, I teach clients about a cycle: **Fear → Avoidance → Anxiety → Stagnation**

The more we avoid the thing we fear, the more anxious we become, and the less we grow. The same is true in this industry. If radio doesn't confront its fear, it will continue to shrink.

I'm not saying we should be reckless. But I *am* saying we should stop being so damn scared of failing that we fail to try.

Failure is not the enemy. Stagnation is.

So how do we flip the format on fear?

We do what the best stations have always done—we take a calculated risk. We give talent room to breathe. We encourage experimentation. We mentor. We lead with vision, not fear.

Let's stop punishing mistakes and start celebrating learning. Let's invite our teams to take initiative. Let's make room for fresh ideas, diverse voices, weird promotions, and bold stunts.

Let's make radio fun again.

Fear doesn't have to win.

We can choose courage instead.

Mike McVay on Embracing Failure

To reinforce this idea from the inside out, we'll feature a reflection from longtime industry leader Mike McVay. He's seen firsthand how fear shows up in programming decisions, in talent development, and in boardroom discussions. His contribution spotlights what it takes to embrace calculated risk and foster long-term resilience—even when the stakes are high.

It would be difficult for anyone who is honest with themselves, and others, to deny having had failure in their lives and careers. The longer you work in a field, the greater the magnitude of your work, the more likely you will have failure on your doorstep. The key to following failure is how you rebound. How do you respond to what didn't succeed as you and others had hoped it would.

Being a consultant since 1984 and having spent 9 years as an Executive Vice President at a large broadcast company during a segment of my consulting career, I've seen and experienced failure along with success. The successes always seem more fleeting than the failures. Success ... you celebrate and move on. Failure ... you stop, regroup, assess, evaluate, and strategize a new plan to accomplish your goal.

Portland, Oregon is a unique market. I know that everyone says their market is unique, but my experience is that Portland truly is unique. They still have hippies on Pioneer Square downtown. People who move there do so because of the lifestyle and the beauty of the area. Those who are natives dislike the "newbies" who they view as ruining what was once amazing. These eccentricities (my word) of the community make it a difficult market for an outsider to understand, and program in a relatable way.

I had two different consulting stints in Portland. Neither went well. It wasn't until I accepted failure, and acknowledged my shortcomings, that the approach I desired to develop for the market worked. The secret was hiring people who knew Portland, were from or had lived there for some time, and who were willing to learn as much as possible about the market. It took me far too long to admit that what had worked for me in other markets wouldn't work in Portland, Oregon.

Jim Rohn Was Right: Failure Brings Clarity

As Jim Rohn said:

"Failure brings clarity and should change your path if it is not the right one. The longer you stay on it, the longer it will take to find your true destiny."

Fear doesn't have to block the road—it can redirect us. If you can identify fear early, you can flip it into curiosity, courage, and action.

Actionable Worksheet: Your Fear-to-Freedom Plan

Step 1: Identify Your Top 3 Career Fears

Name the fears that keep you stuck, silent, or small.

Step 2: Examine the Worst-Case Scenario

What's the absolute worst that could happen if that fear came true? What would you do?

Step 3: Flip the Format

Rewrite your fear:

- ✗ "I'll look stupid if I pitch this."

- ☑ "I have an idea worth hearing, and I'm practicing leadership."

Step 4: Take One Small Brave Action

Pick something you've been avoiding and do it today—even just a little bit.

Final Thoughts: You Decide What Fear Means

You are not a slave to your fear-based programming. You are the programmer.

Each time you act in spite of fear, you weaken its grip. You write a new story. You install a new format.

You're already Badass. This chapter just gave you the science to prove it.

Next Up: The Psychology of Success and Leadership

Chapter 3 will explore how high-performing leaders in radio build resilience, influence, and confidence by knowing themselves.

CHAPTER 3

Reprogramming the Brain for Confidence and Creativity

W.K.R.P. Framework: Winning Mindset

Fear Rewires the Brain — But So Can You

Fear is powerful — but it isn't permanent. And the good news is, your brain is always listening, learning, and adapting. That means you have more control over your confidence and creativity than you might think.

In radio, where performance pressure is real and reinvention is constant, your mindset becomes your operating system. And when fear is running that system, everything slows down.

From neuroscience to personal stories, let's flip the format on the fear-based thinking that keeps you stuck.

The Science of Fear and the Creative Brain

Your brain is hardwired to protect you. That's why fear shows up fast and strong. The amygdala — the brain's alarm system — treats creative risk the same way it treats physical danger.

Fear floods the body with stress hormones like cortisol and adrenaline.

The prefrontal cortex — responsible for logic, reasoning, and creativity — shuts down.

🪨 **Neural pathways of fear** get reinforced every time we avoid risk.

But here's the best part: the brain is neuroplastic. That means it can be retrained.

Every time you practice gratitude, visualize success, or challenge a limiting belief, you're building new mental programming. You're strengthening the confidence circuits in your brain.

Personal Story: From Breakdown to Breakthrough

When I was diagnosed with congestive heart failure, everything I thought I knew about my future vanished. I was forced into stillness. I couldn't work. I couldn't plan. I was terrified.

But that pause taught me to tune in to something deeper. I started a gratitude practice—not because I felt grateful, but because I needed something to anchor me. I wrote down three things every morning. Some days, it was simply, "I'm breathing."

Over time, I felt the shift. My thoughts became less panicked, more hopeful. I visualized myself working again—not in the same way, but in a way that aligned with who I was becoming. I didn't just recover physically—I reprogrammed mentally.

That experience didn't just change my life. It became the foundation for this book.

Apple A Day: Mindset Reset

Just like your favorite radio station, your mindset is broadcasting a frequency. When you wake up and immediately feel dread, worry, or fear—it's time to change the station.

You have control of your dial. Tune in to courage. Tune in to creativity. Tune in to gratitude.

Your brain is listening. Your spirit is responding. And your audience—your coworkers, your clients, your listeners—they all pick up on the frequency you emit.

Change your signal. Change your outcome. You're the DJ of your own mind."

A Learner's Mindset Flips the Frequency

One of the most transformative discoveries I made during my own personal development journey was that I'm a learner. Marcus Buckingham's *Now, Discover Your Strengths* confirmed that my top strength is "Learner." When I teach or coach, I approach it as a student first—absorbing everything I can so I can teach authentically and effectively.

In every coaching program, keynote, and workshop, I return to this idea: to teach is to learn. And to learn is to lead. If you want to flip your mindset, start by feeding it with knowledge—and stay humble enough to keep learning from the people around you.

The Station Between Fear and Faith

The station between fear and faith.

That's where I've been for a while.

There are a lot of things I know how to do. But there are also a lot of things I still need to learn. When fear gets in the way, I have to remind myself to stop and take a breath.

Inhale courage, exhale doubt.

What is the "station between fear and faith?"

It's the transitional place where you haven't quite arrived at confidence, but you've left behind paralysis. It's the signal that hasn't fully tuned in, but you're adjusting your antenna. It's uncomfortable—but necessary.

It's the place of growth.

In radio, sometimes we have to shift frequencies to reach more listeners. Sometimes, we must change formats to stay relevant. Sometimes, we go off the air for maintenance. It doesn't mean the message is gone. It means it's getting stronger.

You may feel like you're stuck—but you're just tuning in.

You're learning a new frequency.

And that takes time.

📻 Stay with it.

Tools to Rewire Your Brain

◯ **Reframe Fear as Information** – What is this fear telling me I care about?

❀ **Create a Confidence Circuit** – Wins log, affirmations, repetition.

🎧 **Use Music and Rhythm to Shift State** – Sound resets mindset.

☒ **Practice Mindfulness and Awareness** – What's the pattern or story?

☐ **Develop a Gratitude Playlist** – Three things daily. Simple but powerful.

⊚ **Visualize Success Before It Happens** – Mental rehearsal = confidence.

The Brain Is a Signal Tower—You're the DJ

Fear might be the default station your brain tunes in to, but that doesn't mean it's the only one available. In fact, you have more control over the dial than you think.

Your brain is a signal tower, constantly broadcasting your thoughts—whether empowering or defeating. Every day, you're spinning tracks on the soundtrack of your life.

🧠 That's why I say: *You're the DJ of your own mind.*

Your brain is like a radio station—you're constantly spinning thoughts, ideas, and beliefs, sending out frequencies into the world that others can pick up. The question is, are you broadcasting positivity, confidence, and resilience—or are you stuck in a loop of fear, self-doubt, and defeat?

Think of your internal dialogue as the playlist you're spinning. Are your thoughts on repeat filled with old regrets, negative assumptions, and worst-case scenarios? Or are you curating empowering messages, lessons learned, and hopeful visions for your future?

Neuroscience tells us that the brain is incredibly plastic—meaning it can change, adapt, and rewire itself through experience and intention. This is called neuroplasticity. It's like having the power to remix your mental playlist at any time.

The more you think a thought, the more you reinforce a neural pathway. If your default mental station is tuned to "I'm not good enough" or "What if I fail?", you're strengthening those tracks in your brain. But the reverse is also true. If you begin to practice thoughts like "I've overcome challenges before" or "I am capable of learning," you are literally rewiring your brain to support success and resilience.

This is why mindset work matters. You have the power to intentionally shift your mental programming. Instead of waiting for your circumstances to change, you can flip the script internally first.

So… what are you playing today on your mental station?

🎧 Flip the format.

🎧 Spin something empowering.

🎧 Be your own mental producer.

🎧 Grab the mic.

🎧 Remix your mindset.

Insider Insight: Mike McVay on Rewiring from the Top

Helping talent overcome fear

We hear the phrase "Stage Fright" thrown around when it comes to theatre, singers on stage, public speaking, and in high profile award presentations. We don't hear it mentioned often around radio performers. It is real and it does happen. It's rooted in not wanting to embarrass ourselves. It comes from expectations that we as personalities have of ourselves. We build up in our heads the way we want to sound, be perceived, accepted, and appreciated.

The rewiring for talent, in overcoming fear, starts with how we see ourselves. There is a certain persona that talent has in their mind of who they are as a performer. When I was on-air in the early days of my career, I modeled myself after those personalities that I most enjoyed listening to and admired. Imitating someone else was a good way to learn, but it didn't allow me to be me on the air. I was "acting" and my fear of failing the performance increased the odds that I would not meet my own expectations. It wasn't until I got tired of "trying" and instead started "doing" that I achieved the performance level I was searching for through my *Air Talent Era*.

Sometimes we must succumb to the realization that our own expectations are too high. Crank it back a notch or two. Accomplish something that brings you the feeling of success. Let that sink in and simmer. Then slowly evolve and grow to where you want to be as a performer. There's a line that Tom Cruise says in the movie "Risky Business" …

"Sometimes you just have to say What the F."

Actionable Worksheet: Your Brain Reset Plan

☑ **Step 1:** Identify One Fear-Based Loop

☑ **Step 2:** Flip the Format

☑ **Step 3:** Choose a Tool and commit for one week

☑ **Step 4:** Track the Shift and journal your growth

Final Thoughts: Tune Your Brain Like a Station

Your brain is like a signal tower. It broadcasts what you feed it. If you want confidence and creativity, you have to program them in.

Every small practice counts. You don't need to be perfect—you just need to be consistent.

If you've made it this far, you're already Licensed2BBadass.

■ **Next Up:** In Chapter 4, we'll explore how to align your goals with your values and live in integrity—on the air and off.

PART 2

K — Know Thyself

Chapters 4–6

CHAPTER 4

Own Your Identity – Strengths Over Self-Doubt

W.K.R.P. Framework: K – Know Thyself

Why Knowing Yourself Is Your Greatest Advantage

In radio—and in life—people often wait for permission to be themselves. They try to fit in, mimic others, or mute their instincts in hopes of being accepted or respected. But here's the truth: the most magnetic leaders, creative talents, and successful professionals know exactly who they are—and they lean into it.

If fear hijacks your creativity, self-doubt is what steals your confidence. The antidote? Clarity. Clarity of purpose. Clarity of strengths. Clarity of voice. When you know who you are, fear has less room to thrive.

In radio, we talk about "voice" all the time. But your truest voice isn't just how you sound on-air—it's how you show up in every room, every decision, every moment. When you stop hiding and start owning your identity, everything changes.

Personal Story: Owning My Voice in a Male-Dominated Industry

I grew up in radio. Literally. My dad built our family station from scratch, and I was there—from the filing cabinets to the FCC logs.

But I was also a woman in a business that didn't always make room for women at the table.

For years, I second-guessed myself. I asked for approval. I deferred to others. I played small.

But when I finally realized that my unique experience—growing up in the business, surviving health crises, earning a psychology degree—was actually *my edge,* I began to lead differently. I stopped apologizing for being different and started using it as my greatest strength.

Who Are You in the Studio?

From the "Know Thyself" Files

I had spent a couple of hours in the studio that day—alone and quiet.

I needed to feel the energy of the station—the heartbeat of broadcasting. I sat in the chair, turned on the mic, and didn't speak a word. I just sat in silence, listening to the hum of the board, watching the lights blink back at me like a familiar rhythm.

But then something happened:

I **remembered** something.

Something I had forgotten for a while.

I **belonged** there.

The studio felt like home. Like identity. Like purpose.

You see, it's easy to forget who you are when the world tells you to be someone else. It's easy to lose sight of your value when every rating, review, or job posting whispers that you're too old, too new, too bold, too something.

But inside that booth—surrounded by soundproof walls and the ghosts of a thousand broadcasts—I remembered.

I'm a **storyteller**.

I'm a **broadcaster**.

I'm a **guide**.

The mic may have been off, but my purpose was fully on.

So, I challenge you:

🎙 Who are *you* in the studio?

When the mic is off, do you still believe in your message?

When the room is empty, do you still trust your voice?

When nobody's clapping or commenting or promoting, do you still know your worth?

That day in the studio became a turning point for me—not because I said anything, but because I **remembered everything**.

Identity doesn't come from validation.

It comes from *remembrance*.

From *alignment*.

From *knowing who you are*—especially when no one is watching.

So, take a moment, maybe even today. Sit in your "studio," wherever that may be.

Feel the hum.

Close your eyes.

And ask yourself:

◔ Who am I—really—when the noise is gone?

The answer might just change everything.

Apple a Day: Stop Hating Yourself for What You Aren't

"What are your strengths? Has anyone ever pointed them out to you—or have you ever really thought about them? I'm good at writing, dancing, being creative, helping people, and coming up with solutions to problems. I'm not great at crafts. I don't love cooking. But I'm grateful for what I am good at."

"Stop comparing yourself to other people and their strengths. Stop hating yourself for everything that you aren't. Start loving yourself for everything that you are."

"Make a list of your strengths. Be grateful for each one. Then go out and be fruitful."

Imposter Syndrome: The Quiet Crisis in Broadcasting

"In radio, confidence is currency."

It's what earns you the mic, sells the pitch, and rallies the team. But behind the on-air charisma and sharp production, many professionals suffer silently from a thief called imposter syndrome.

They fear they're one mistake away from being "found out." They second-guess their instincts, dismiss their accomplishments, and assume they've somehow fooled everyone into believing they belong.

📻 "I didn't earn this role—I just got lucky."

📻 "Sooner or later, someone's going to realize I'm not qualified."

📻 "I can't ask for help—that'll prove I'm not good enough."

These thoughts don't discriminate. It doesn't matter if you're brand new or a 30-year vet. Imposter syndrome is an identity crisis, not a competence issue. It grows in isolation and thrives in silence.

Imposter syndrome doesn't care about your resume. It's not about talent. It's about perception—your perception of yourself.

Why This Matters

Radio is built on voices. But when internal voices are filled with doubt, fear, and shame, even the loudest personalities shrink. We lose innovation. We lose authenticity. We lose leaders.

The cost?

Talented people burn out, play small, or walk away altogether. They defer to louder voices or hide behind perfectionism. They confuse humility with invisibility.

How to Flip the Format on Imposter Syndrome

✔ Normalize the Doubt

Feeling unsure doesn't make you unqualified. It makes you human. Self-doubt often signals growth, not inadequacy.

✔ Validate through Values

When you ground your confidence in your values—rather than likes, applause, or job titles—you become less shakable.

✔ Feedback Loops, Not Echo Chambers

Mentorship, peer reviews, and open team feedback create safe places to grow. When people feel seen and supported, imposter syndrome loses its grip.

✅ Affirm Your Identity

Name your strengths. Own your wins. You're not "faking it"— you've been showing up and earning it.

"When people know who they are and what they bring, they stop performing—and start transforming."

Insider Insight: Mike McVay on Identity in Broadcasting

There is a strength that comes with confidence and a belief in yourself that overcomes imposter syndrome. It is a fine line between *confidence* and *conceit.* Knowing thyself, as Kelly suggests, is important. Because I know my limitations, I am cautious when I extend them. I know what I am capable of, and what I'm not capable of doing. That doesn't mean that I won't try things that I've never done, but "reason" is a part of my decision process.

Knowing who you are and what you stand for is important, too. There's a scene in the movie Bull Durham, starring Kevin Costner, Susan Sarandon, and Timothy Robbins, that I like to play for air talent when I first begin coaching them. This scene is one where Sarandon's character announces to Costner and Robbins that she's going to pick one of them to be her boyfriend for the minor league baseball season. Costner objects and stands to leave the situation, to which Sarandon asks, "Where are you going Crash?" He says "I'm leaving. I don't believe that you can apply quantum physics to matters of the heart." To which she asks, "Then what do you believe in?" Kevin Costner's character responds with a monologue that is specific and delivered passionately. Among those specific was that "Astroturf should be outlawed, a ground ball through the gap is more majestic than a Home Run, Lee Harvey Oswald acted alone and there's nothing better than a warm bath, surrounded by candles, on a rainy day."

The actors in Bull Durham had a script writer. In real life we don't. However, the very best talent knows who they are, what they believe, what they will do and what they won't do, and what they're good at and what they're not.

That movie clip shows me to be able to ask the talent who they are so that my coaching is appropriate for them. You have to know who you are and what you believe to be confident in being who you want to be.

📝 Reclaim Your Identity:

- List 3 moments where you made a real impact in your role.
- What did those moments say about your strengths?
- What feedback have you been ignoring or brushing off? Re-read it. Own it.

Actionable Worksheet: Strengths Over Self-Doubt

✅ Step 1: Identify Your Strengths

Write down five strengths that make you a great professional, leader, or creator.

✅ Step 2: Track the Impact

For each strength, note how it has positively impacted a project, person, or performance.

☑ Step 3: Flip the Script

Rewrite one self-doubt you've been carrying. Turn it into a strength-based affirmation.

Example:

✗ "I'm not as experienced as others."

☑ "My fresh perspective is exactly what this team needs."

☑ Step 4: Practice Confidence Daily

Choose a morning mantra, gratitude practice, or 5-minute visualization to remind yourself who you are.

Final Thoughts: Stop Asking for Permission to Be Yourself

The world doesn't need another imitation. It needs you.

Your voice. Your story. Your strengths.

When you stop performing and start *believing*, you reclaim the mic. You direct the signal. You own your identity—and the power that comes with it.

🚀 You've been Licensed2BBadass all along. Now act like it.

Next Up: Licensed2BBadass Mindset Shift

In Chapter 5, we'll dive into the power of owning your mindset— how reframing your thoughts can rewire your results.

CHAPTER 5

The Truth About Confidence

W.K.R.P. Framework: Knowing Thyself

Confidence Isn't a Trait—It's a Tool

Let's bust a myth right now: Confidence isn't something you're born with. It's something you build.

The truth is, most people in the radio industry—whether on-air, in management, or behind the scenes—struggle with self-doubt at some point. That polished, professional voice you hear on the air? It might be masking a swirling storm of uncertainty.

Confidence is not the absence of fear. It's the decision to act anyway.

Real confidence is knowing who you are and standing in that truth—even when your voice shakes. Even when others doubt you. Even when you doubt yourself.

Don't Let Your Inner Critic Speak Louder Than Your Passion

There's a voice in my head I've been trying to ignore.

It's the one that says, "You're not good enough. You're not ready. You're going to fail."

You know that voice. We all do. It's the inner critic that shows up when we try something new. The one that echoes past criticism and amplifies fear.

But here's what I've learned—sometimes the volume of your passion has to drown out the noise of your inner critic.

I was preparing a keynote speech and started spiraling. "Who do you think you are?" "They've probably heard all this before." "You're not as smart as they think."

But then I stopped. I took a deep breath. I reminded myself: This message matters. I have something to share. I've worked hard. I've earned my place.

The critic never goes away. But it doesn't get to run the show.

So when that voice creeps in—check the volume. Then turn up the station in your heart that's playing your purpose loud and clear.

Radio Needs an Attitude Adjustment

Although I'm not immune to the ongoing challenges that the radio industry faces, my primary focus is on the people inside the industry. My broadcast career was derailed in 2006 when I was hospitalized suddenly, suffering from an undiagnosed heart arrhythmia that led to heart failure.

The life-threatening heart disease that almost took my life and derailed my career was the catalyst in the decision to flip my radio career path and study psychology. I wanted to help people in more ways than I could as a radio executive. I began graduate school studies, then completed an internship as a Behavioral Health professional. I became a licensed psychotherapist in 2012, specializing in depression, anxiety, stress, and the behavioral health issues that plague 25-30% of the U.S. population.

Consider that statistic and its direct impact on you and your organization!

Whatever role or title you have, take some time to consider the people you directly work with, lead, or supervise. Twenty-five percent of the U.S. population suffers from symptoms of depression, anxiety and stress, creating a huge financial impact on businesses. This translates to one in four people on your team. Possibly even you. These conditions may be undiagnosed and untreated.

I 've spent a lot of time having confidential, frank dialogue with numerous radio professionals from every department and management level. My intent was to discover practical ways to truly bring value to this industry that I love. Those conversations allowed me to assess the state of mind of radio professionals, and revealed that there is one main problem that is being neglected …

FEAR. More specifically; fear of failure.

The trouble, turmoil and transitions in radio with so many mergers, acquisitions, format changes, ownership changes, and disruptions in media have shaken radio to its core. People are afraid to take risks, afraid to speak up, afraid of getting fired or not promoted, afraid to stay, afraid to go, afraid that the radio business is failing. Hopelessness and fear set in.

Fear paralyzes you. Stress is a result of FEAR-based emotions. Left untreated, the effects of stress have a significant negative impact on your health as well as your relationships.

Fear impairs your ability to communicate effectively, and lead your company and the industry to the success and profits you want to achieve.

Sales training and vanilla leadership alone won't get radio where it needs to go. The radio industry is heavily reliant upon the human component; automation, syndication and more consolidation are not the answers. Living, breathing humans are what will keep radio alive and thriving into the future – unless we all want to turn our licenses in and become internet-based media companies.

Radio's healthy workplace begins in the C-suite – fresh perspective.

When I finished my graduate school training in psychology, I had to complete more than 3,000 hours in the field of Behavioral Health as an intern before I could qualify to take the grueling and lengthy set of tests to become licensed as a psychotherapist.

For a period of time I was employed as a psychotherapist with an organization providing free mental health services to the low-income population. The department I was assigned to work in was Late Life Depression, which offered a program for seniors. This job also had a marketing component, and I found that my years of experience in radio really helped my ability to do research, find the right resources, and conduct outreach, which enabled me to create and develop programs to increase awareness and engagement with this population. One of the services I offered was a depression support group at a senior citizen center. The participants of the group affectionately named it "The Blues Club."

What does this have to do with the mental and emotional state in broadcasting?

When I created the program for the community of seniors, it evolved out of a need to improve their lives. They would come to the center in hope of finding fun activities to keep them engaged, meet new friends, play games, and go on outings. They wanted to get out of their homes and find helpful resources to stay active and healthy.

But there was a glaring problem. Everybody was so negative and depressed. They would sit around and talk about their aches and pains, how the economy was suffering, and the rising cost of healthcare, among other things. They complained all the time, and found many others who felt negative and depressed. This only promoted a more negative atmosphere. They weren't achieving the goals that brought them to the senior center in the first place. Sure, they found camaraderie; their consensus was that life is hard. Life is miserable. Depression is inevitable. We've all failed at life.

By implementing a supportive system with specific tools to increase positivity in how they think, feel and behave, the individuals who participated in the group saw significant improvement in their well-being and overall lives.

Negativity only increases negativity.

How do you begin your day? Today is an ideal time to take inventory of your own mood as well as the mindset around you. Look at things from a helicopter view. Are you excited to get out of bed and get going with your to-do list, or do you wake up feeling anxious and drag your feet while asking yourself, "What crisis is going to happen today?" How does your immediate team measure up? Is there a lot of negative talk around the office?

Positive thinking alone doesn't cure a crisis, but it will help you navigate through it and aid you in developing better solutions to the problems you face. Your attitude will largely determine the attitude of your team members. But it doesn't happen overnight.

It takes effort to shift your mindset and adjust your attitude from negative to positive.

According to Strategic Coaching founder and psychotherapist Cloe Madanes who has trained coaches all over the world including Tony Robbins, there are six universal human needs:

- Certainty; feeling secure; knowing what's going to happen next
- Uncertainty; variety; change
- Significance
- Love/Connection
- Growth
- Contribution

When you strategically take care of your team by meeting at least two of these needs, you will see a positive shift in direction. Remember, people don't quit jobs; they quit bosses. Of course, nobody is indispensable, but it's more productive and cost- effective to keep our already-established teams happy, healthy and productive, than to expect them to function well in an atmosphere of constant unrest, turmoil and turnover.

Confident Leadership

The people inside radio stations are the real assets of the organization. Sure, you own some licenses, properties and transmitters, but the true assets lie in radio's creativity, innovation, the ability to inform and entertain your audiences, and bring value to your advertisers. You serve your local community and have fought the battle of remaining relevant in the age of digital media. But there is more to be done for radio to pull out of the predicted flat revenue growth in 2018, and to thrive.

Fear and negativity block creativity and innovation. Period.

Leadership in the radio industry must change frequency! The status quo will not promote growth. A "this is how we've always done it" mentality is detrimental to any business.

The Confidence Formula: Identity + Action + Support

There's a formula I've taught my coaching clients for years. It's not magic, but it works:

Confidence = Identity + Action + Support

- **Identity**: Know who you are, what you value, and what you're capable of.
- **Action**: Do the thing—even when you're afraid.
- **Support**: Surround yourself with people who see your light, especially when you can't.

When you know your purpose, take aligned action, and get consistent encouragement, confidence compounds.

Insider Insight: Mike McVay on Cultivating Confidence in Radio

When I first arrived in Wheeling, WV. market, it was as a Program Director and Morning Talent on an Adult Contemporary station. The station itself was in a neighboring community. Moundsville, WV. I was fortunate to work for an Operations Manager who had been on-air in bigger markets and had a level of business and broadcast experience that I lacked. He taught me to be confident by giving me the opportunity to perform, allowing me to fall, pick myself up, dust off, and get back at it. Realizing that the times I fell were learning experiences, helped me to lessen my fear of falling. The repercussions for my imbalance were limited. Never reprimanded. Always taught. The confident individual I grew into started there, with guidance and encouragement.

We pass mile markers in our career that add to our confidence. Performing well in Moundsville led to performing well in Wheeling, and then Charleston, Los Angeles, Louisville, and Cleveland. The success we experience should be learning moments. Cause for celebration, but not a reason to stop pushing forward.

One of the most seminal moments in my career came while in Wheeling, WV as a PD/Morning Talent. The afternoon talent on the station had worked in Pittsburgh, PA and performed at a high level. Because I grew up in Western Pennsylvania, my dream was to work in Pittsburgh. Once while bemoaning my frustration that I was still in Wheeling, the Afternoon talent said to me "The difference between you and the talent in Pittsburgh is that you're here and they're there. That's it. It's the same job."

I remembered that a few years later when I found myself working in Los Angeles.

Truth Check: You Don't Have to Feel Ready to Be Ready

One of the most powerful lessons I've learned is that confidence often comes *after* the action—not before.

You start the podcast and find your voice along the way.

You pitch the idea and realize you had what it takes all along.

You step on stage and become the speaker you hoped you'd be.

Stop waiting to feel ready. Start showing up.

Actionable Worksheet: Strengthen Your Confidence Circuit

✓ Step 1: Identify Your Confidence Leaks

What situations make you shrink? Who makes you doubt yourself? Name them.

✓ Step 2: Rewrite the Script

Choose one recurring negative thought and flip it.

✗ "I always mess up when I present."

✓ "Every time I speak, I grow stronger and clearer."

✓ Step 3: Take a Brave Action

Do something small that scares you. Speak up in a meeting. Share your idea. Post that blog.

✓ Step 4: Ask for Feedback

Find someone you trust and ask what they see as your strengths.

Final Thoughts: Own the Mic

Confidence isn't given—it's earned. Through repetition. Through risk. Through realigning your inner voice with your outer purpose.

You've already got the voice. Now trust it. Use it. Own it.

In radio and in life, confidence is your frequency.

Dial it in.

And don't let the static stop you.

Next Up: Respect, Teamwork, and Culture Building

Chapter 6 explores how to foster healthy dynamics, mutual support, and shared success in your station, your team, and your leadership journey.

CHAPTER 6

Why Respect and Teamwork Are Non-Negotiable

🔑 W.K.R.P. Framework: Know Thyself

Respect, Teamwork, and Culture Building

Great stations aren't just built on strong programming or big sales. They are built on strong relationships. No amount of ratings or revenue can sustain a toxic culture. The foundation of any high-performing team is built on respect and collaboration.

I've been in countless studios, sales pits, and station offices. I can tell almost immediately what kind of culture exists by watching how people interact:

✔️ Do they acknowledge each other with genuine warmth?

✔️ Are they laughing, exchanging ideas, or walking on eggshells?

✔️ Is the air filled with creativity or tension?

Culture is felt before it's spoken. And it is shaped moment by moment by how people treat each other.

At one station I consulted with, programming and sales were locked in a constant battle. There was a clear "us vs. them" mentality. Sales thought programming didn't understand business. Programming believed sales only cared about money. Both departments had talent, but their inability to work together stalled every project. The ratings suffered, revenue dipped, and leadership blamed the market.

When I intervened, we didn't start with strategy. We started with respect. We brought both sides into a room and asked one question:

"What does the other department do that you appreciate?"

Silence at first. Then, stories began to surface. Small acknowledgments. A breakthrough. That simple question turned tension into connection. Within three months, the tone changed. Within six, the numbers followed.

Personal Story: The KVVQ Culture We Built

When my family built KVVQ-FM in Victorville, we didn't just create a radio station. We built a culture from scratch. Everyone wore multiple hats. I did traffic and billing, ran errands, cleaned, and recorded public service announcements. I learned every aspect of the business, but more importantly, I learned what it took to create a supportive, respectful team.

Nobody said, *"That's not my job."* If something needed to be done, we stepped up. When someone was overwhelmed, we helped. That spirit became our identity. It wasn't about hierarchy. It was about teamwork.

There was a sense of pride and purpose. People didn't just show up to work. They showed up to be part of something. That kind of culture doesn't happen by accident. It is built intentionally, from the top down and the ground up.

Victorville Blog Entry: Lead From the Inside Out

I've always said that good leadership is about knowing your people. Not just managing them, but truly knowing them. I once coached a station manager who had a revolving door of staff and couldn't figure out why morale was tanking. I asked one question: 'When's the last time you had a real conversation with your staff about something other than work?' He couldn't remember.

That's the problem. Leaders forget that people bring their whole selves to work—their families, their worries, their passions. When you treat staff like widgets, they act like machines. When you treat them like people, they become invested. They bring ideas, energy, and commitment. That's culture.

Culture isn't a memo. It's a mood. It's built in the in-between moments—grabbing coffee, walking through the halls, the way you say good morning. It's built by how you respond to mistakes and how often you say thank you.

When we lead from the inside out, we shift the focus from control to connection. And that's where real leadership lives.

What Does Your Studio Culture Sound Like?

I was consulting with a radio group when I was invited to observe an aircheck session between the PD and a new morning show talent. I sat quietly in the back of the room and listened to the critique and feedback the Program Director was offering the new hire. As I listened, I became more and more uncomfortable and even confused. The critique was harsh and sarcastic, and not at all constructive. The new talent remained quiet and expressionless—taking it all in. The session ended, the talent left the room, and the

PD turned to me and asked what I thought. I said, "Honestly, I thought it was abusive." He was surprised and asked what I meant. I explained, "It was mean and sarcastic. There wasn't a single helpful or encouraging comment offered, only criticism, mockery, and put-downs. I'm shocked at how this new hire handled it so stoically. You may have crushed this person's confidence without realizing it."

The PD insisted that he was only "joking around," but that's the problem. That was *his* culture. He didn't see how damaging it could be to someone else.

I didn't say anything else. It was his team, not mine. But I made a mental note of the environment, because the studio culture wasn't just what happened in that aircheck. That sarcastic, "tough-guy" persona was evident in all areas of the station—from the way the sales managers spoke to their teams, to the morning banter in the hallway, to the way engineering responded to requests. Everyone had adopted a survival mechanism: either fight, flight, or freeze.

The culture of a radio station—especially in the studio—is heard on the air. You can *feel* a good culture through the speakers. You can *sense* a toxic culture too. It's in the tone, the energy, the chemistry. You can tell when people genuinely enjoy their work, feel supported, and are encouraged to grow. And you can tell when they're just going through the motions, or worse—working in fear.

It's time we ask ourselves: What does our studio culture sound like?

Apple a Day: What Are You Broadcasting?

Every day, you're broadcasting something—even when you're not behind the mic. Your tone, your attitude, your energy—they all go out on your internal frequency. Are you spreading calm or chaos? Are you lifting people up or tuning them out?

There was a time when I realized my burnout was leaking out. I wasn't shouting, but I was short. I wasn't rude, but I was rushed. That energy filled the room. And it wasn't until a colleague asked if I was okay that I realized I needed to tune back in to myself.

Leadership isn't about always being 'on.' It's about being aligned. If your internal station is broadcasting negativity, fear, or resentment—others will pick up the signal. Reset your frequency. Choose your mindset. And remember that you're a transmitter of culture.

Today's Reflection: What signal are you sending?

Culture Is the New Format

Building Morale and Teamwork in a Small Market

What began as a business rescue project became a personal and professional transformation for everyone involved. We couldn't afford egos, turf wars, or rigid 'that's not my job' attitudes. Instead, we rolled up our sleeves—every single one of us. I coached, I sold, I wrote copy. Our board op doubled as the morning guy. The market manager pitched in with remotes. It was all hands on deck.

That's when it clicked: building a team isn't about hierarchy—it's about humility. We didn't need a mission statement hanging on the wall. We were living it. When you show your team that you're in the trenches with them, that you see them, that you respect what they're doing—it ignites a new kind of loyalty.

Respect Starts at the Top

The studios and offices we work in—no matter how big or small—are still cultures, and cultures are led. If leadership models respect, inclusion, and collaboration, it trickles down. But if there's blame, favoritism, or unchecked egos, it doesn't matter how many HR seminars you host—your culture will be toxic.

The fastest way to ruin morale was to ignore the people who made the place tick. Sales reps, front desk staff, street teamers—they're all part of the success. When respect is uneven, so is effort.

Do You Know Your Team?

You know what's great about radio? It takes a team. There's nothing like seeing engineers, salespeople, on-air talent, and traffic managers working in harmony to make the product shine. I've always believed that the best broadcast teams are like jazz bands—everyone has a solo, but they also know when to back each other up. That's respect.

Want to build culture? Start by listening. Not just to the music or the breaks—but to your team.

Insider Insight: Mike McVay's Perspective on Team Culture

The business of broadcasting has changed so dramatically since the pandemic. There was a time when I could tell the culture of a radio station the minute I walked in the front door. If the receptionist was cheerful, the building felt bright and happy, you heard music in the lobby, and laughter down the hallways ... it was a winning culture. If it was the opposite of that in every one of the aforementioned areas, then you could expect that the culture in the building was bad.

Today with many jobs being performed remotely, fewer and fewer radio stations even have a receptionist. Technology has allowed teleporting, encouraged digital distribution or prizing, communication, copy writing and production. Every job in a radio station can be done elsewhere today. That puts an onus on those in leadership today to have regular communication with their team members. The connection can be in a group, one on one, or both at varying times. The more remote your group, the more important it is that you have regular communication.

Along the way I've had several positions that were in addition to my role at McVay Media Consulting. I was aware that there were some cultural issues at one of those positions. My predecessor communicated poorly, but insisted that everything (I mean everything) be cleared through them before a department head or employee could take action. They then often disappeared and as such requests went unrecognized. Another senior executive was terrible at returning E-Mail. Internal communication was poor. There was criticism of performance, but seldom ever was their praise. The hallways felt as if individuals should be shackled and hanging from the walls.

My decision to *lead by example* quickly caught the attention of the team. I never asked anyone on the Content Team to do something that I wouldn't do myself. Sometimes I did such things purposely to show my humility and to let them know that I saw not as being above the job at hand. I returned every E-mail I received before I went to bed at night. I empowered department heads and format captains to do their jobs, but I never let them feel as if they were acting without my support. We started celebrating successes. We analyzed failures without blame, but rather took an investigative look to allow for strategy discussions. We created Action Plans and assigned tasks, deadlines, and encouraged collaboration. The culture changed. It took a long time, but it is a different world today than it was then.

Reflection: Respect and Teamwork Self-Inventory

Instead of a checklist, take a moment for personal insight:

☑ When was the last time you praised a teammate without being prompted?

☑ Who on your team might be feeling invisible right now?

☑ How can you contribute to the culture you want to be part of?

Write it down. Act on it. Reflect on it weekly.

Actionable Worksheet: Culture Builder's Challenge

Step 1: Identify a "quiet contributor" on your team—someone whose work supports the whole but rarely gets praise.

Step 2: Acknowledge them—privately or publicly. Write a note. Send an email. Mention it in a meeting.

Step 3: Host a five-minute team check-in this week. No agenda. Just ask, *"What's one thing going well?"*

Step 4: Commit to one culture-building behavior to practice daily. (Ex: Gratitude, check-ins, encouragement)

Final Thoughts: You Shape the Culture

Culture isn't HR's job. It's everyone's job. Especially yours.

Whether you're on the air, in the back office, or managing the market, your attitude, your tone, and your daily choices shape the environment.

The good news? You have more power than you think.

Lead with respect. Invite connection. Build something people want to belong to.

📻 And the culture you build today will echo on every frequency tomorrow.

PART 3

R — Resilience, Responsibility & Respect

Chapters 7–9

CHAPTER 7

Building Resilience and Managing Setbacks

W.K.R.P. Framework: Resilience

Why Resilience Matters in Radio — and in Life

Resilience isn't just about bouncing back. It's about adapting, learning, and moving forward despite adversity. In an industry like radio, setbacks are inevitable:

- A format change that alienates loyal listeners.
- A sudden job loss due to corporate restructuring.
- A major industry shift that forces reinvention.

The most successful people in this business aren't the ones who never fail — they're the ones who learn to recover quickly, reframe setbacks, and pivot with purpose. Resilience isn't a personality trait. It's a skill. And it can be developed.

The Wrong Shoes

It was 108 degrees, and I had the wrong shoes.

You see, when I planned this particular leg of the RV trip, I wasn't planning to hike across a jagged desert parking lot. I thought I'd just be unhooking the trailer, grabbing a cold drink, and catching up on emails from the air-conditioned comfort of the RV.

But plans change.

A miscommunication with the RV park manager meant I had to relocate the trailer—twice. I was sweaty, sunburned, and irritated, trying to line up the trailer perfectly while wearing thin sandals better suited for a beach day. My feet were burning. My attitude? Even worse.

But then it struck me: I couldn't change the weather. I couldn't change the gravel. I couldn't even change the fact that I was now late for a virtual appointment. But I *could* change my shoes. And I could change my mindset.

I took a deep breath, swapped my sandals for sneakers, grabbed a bottle of water, and laughed at the absurdity of it all. Just like that, the frustration melted a bit. I was still hot and tired—but I wasn't miserable anymore.

Sometimes, resilience means literally changing your shoes.

Sometimes, it means laughing through the discomfort.

Sometimes, it means slowing down, adjusting the plan, and reminding yourself that you've survived worse.

That day didn't go as planned. But it reminded me that discomfort is often temporary, and the stories we tell ourselves about how hard things are... well, they can either defeat us or teach us.

I chose the lesson.

Apple A Day: Resilience Is the Key to Bouncing Back

Let's talk about *resilience*. It's not about being invincible—it's about being flexible.

Life throws curveballs. Disappointments. Rejections. Health issues. Setbacks. But resilience is the skill we cultivate when we *bounce back* instead of breaking down.

You've probably been through something tough before—something you weren't sure you'd get through—but look at you. You're here. Still standing.

The key is to stop asking, "Why is this happening to me?" and start asking, "What is this here to teach me?"

Resilient people reframe failure as feedback. They learn. They adjust. They stay open. They forgive themselves and others. They move forward, even if it's one tiny step at a time.

So today, take a moment to reflect:

- ✔ When have you shown resilience?

- ✔ How did you grow because of it?

- ✔ What did you learn?

This is your reminder that you're stronger than you think.

Pivot Points in Radio Careers

I was a second-generation broadcaster and had a long and successful career in radio, working with my dad who founded and built small-market radio stations. We had built a consulting firm as FCC Compliance Specialists after he sold his stations. In 2005, I was preparing for a career change when I was diagnosed with a serious health condition. That's when I found myself at a professional and personal crossroads.

I remember the moment vividly, as I was laying in the emergency room, digesting the news of my health crisis. It was more than just a diagnosis; it was a derailment. I had wanted to expand my horizons and pursue station ownership or executive leadership on my own. But this forced me to stop. To reflect. To reset.

It was at that moment that I realized how drastically life can shift. And how little control we really have over the timing of it.

I was scared. I was angry. I was grieving the career I thought I was going to have.

But eventually, I chose to see it as a pivot point.

I went back to school and earned a Master's Degree in Psychology. I became a licensed Marriage and Family Therapist. And I leaned into my desire to help others navigate their own life transitions— whether personal or professional.

That's why I'm so passionate about supporting those in the radio industry as they face similar pivot points. Whether it's the sale of a station, a format flip, a layoff, a health crisis, or just the feeling of being stuck and unfulfilled, these moments matter.

They are invitations.

To reevaluate what you want. To rediscover your purpose. To reinvent your next chapter.

If you're on the radio and find yourself standing at a fork in the road, I get it. I've been there. And I can tell you this:

There's life beyond the mic.

There's growth beyond the grind.

And sometimes, the greatest success comes not from staying the course, but from having the courage to change it.

Insider Insight – Mike McVay

There have been a couple pivot points in my career. None that took me away from broadcasting, but several that certainly changed my trajectory and put me in a position of moving my family around the country in search of work. Given the benefit of 20/20 hindsight, the experiences were all beneficial to me later in my career. It broadened my perspective and enabled me to relate to what others were going through at the time.

One such situation was taking a job for three days and then returning to my previous position. I was made aware of a great opportunity in a beautiful market where just about anyone would like to live. I didn't really want to leave my previous job, but there was more money, a company car and other such benefits. I took a job for the compensation and "bennies." Which wasn't the right job for me and truth be told, not for them.

Once I'd accepted the new position, but before I departed, senior management at the company I was working for, and the market manager, flew into a location where my wife and I were vacationing with her family. A preplanned vacation before I'd accepted another position and took the job. They matched the offer from the new employer. I'd not signed anything. I could've backed out quietly. Instead I felt an obligation to honor my word and continued on the path to move. Three days in, it became clear that their way of operating was different than what I expected, and I made a call that got me my old job back.

To be fair to the station, they hired a stellar Program Director after me who performed quite well for them. The job was a great job and the people were really good people. It wasn't a job I truly wanted and I allowed the "Bright Lights" to influence me. The pivotal moment was that this potential "career killer" lifted me in the company I was planning to depart. My responsibilities expanded. They taught me the sales side of the business, and it helped me get my first General Manager job. It also brought caution with it for future career moves. I never mistrusted my instincts after that.

☑ Worksheet: Resilience Self-Check
Step 1: Recall a Professional Setback

📝 What happened? How did you react? How did you recover?

Step 2: Reframe the Narrative

🔄 What was the lesson? What new strength emerged from that challenge?

Step 3: Identify Your Triggers

⚠️ What situations test your resilience most? What thoughts arise?

Step 4: Create a Resilience Ritual

⚖️ A daily habit or practice that keeps you grounded and prepared (e.g., journaling, walking, reflection).

Step 5: Acknowledge Your Growth

🦴 List 3 ways you've bounced back and what you learned.

Final Thoughts: Keep Getting Up

Resilience is not about pretending things don't hurt. It's about *deciding* to grow from the pain.

When things fall apart, your first job isn't to rebuild perfectly—it's to breathe. To stand. To choose one next step.

Radio is an industry of reinvention. So is life.

When you're in a tough spot, remember:

You've made it through 100% of your hardest days so far.

You can make it through this one, too.

You've been *Licensed2BBadass* all along.

CHAPTER 8

The Power of Responsibility in Leadership

WKRP Pillar: Resilience, Responsibility, Respect

Own the Job, Not Just the Title

Leadership in radio—or any industry—isn't about claiming a title. It's about taking ownership. True responsibility shows up not only in crisis but in the consistency of everyday decisions. When fear creeps in, many hide behind job descriptions. But flipping the format on fear requires stepping up and showing up, even when it's uncomfortable.

There was a time when I was managing multiple stations with a skeleton staff and a tight budget. Everyone wore multiple hats. Some leaned in and took initiative. Others avoided responsibility like it was contagious. The difference between surviving and thriving? Responsibility.

Be the Boss of Yourself

When I was managing the cluster in Victorville, it was always a delicate dance of encouragement and enforcement. There was a day I walked into the building and it felt... off. Not one person greeted me when I walked through the door. That wasn't normal.

I paused at the front desk. The receptionist had her head down and mumbled a quick hello. I walked the hallway—sales offices dark, production room empty, no laughter from the air studio. My stomach tightened.

One of my team members finally popped out of the break room and said, "We thought you weren't coming in today."

"Why would that matter?" I asked.

That one question led to a team meeting later that afternoon. I reminded them that I wasn't the pulse of the station—they were. If their responsibility hinged on whether or not I showed up, we were in trouble.

Leadership means being accountable whether your boss is watching or not. That day was a reset. They stepped up. And so did I.

🍎 Apple A Day: Responsibility Builds Respect

Today's insight is on **responsibility.** *It's easy to shift blame. It's easy to say, "That's not my job." It's even easier to wait for someone else to fix the problem.*

But the most respected people in your organization? They take responsibility even when they don't have to. They don't step over the trash in the hallway. They don't wait for the email reminder. They lean in.

Responsibility isn't about perfection. It's about ownership.

Ask yourself:

- Where can I take more ownership in my daily tasks?
- How do I respond when something goes wrong?
- Do I look for solutions—or excuses?

Take action: *Today, find one area where you can take initiative before you're asked. And if something goes sideways, own your part. That's how trust is built.*

The Chain Reaction of Accountability

Responsibility is contagious—but so is avoidance. When one team member steps up and owns a problem, it creates a ripple effect. The same is true when someone drops the ball.

A former colleague used to say, *"Don't bring me problems—bring me ownership."* That mantra changed the way we all approached our work. When something went wrong in traffic logs, we didn't just toss the blame at a new hire or automation. We diagnosed the issue, fixed the root, and built a checklist to prevent it again.

Responsibility means going upstream to find the leak—not just mopping up the water.

Radio Leaders Who Walk the Talk

I have worked in radio a long time, long enough to remember a time when station managers led the team with integrity, empathy, and a clear purpose. They knew how to walk the talk.

Back then, radio was not only about profit margins or ratings battles—it was also about community, loyalty, and cultivating talent. Leaders were visible. They walked the halls and spoke with the staff. They didn't hide behind closed doors or rely solely on analytics to make decisions.

When I reflect on what made those leaders different, it wasn't just their business acumen. It was their presence. They were *there*. Not just in the corner office, but in the studio, the break room, the sales pit. They asked questions. They listened. They gave feedback. And, most importantly, they led by example.

I remember one general manager who made it a point to show up to every morning show launch. Not because he needed to micromanage, but because he wanted the team to know they were supported. When sales needed a push, he sat in on strategy meetings—not to dictate, but to contribute. When engineering faced a crisis, he didn't just send an email—he walked down the hall and asked what they needed. That kind of leadership instilled trust.

Unfortunately, not every leader operates this way. Some hide behind memos and delegate culture-building to HR. Others focus exclusively on data and ignore the emotional and psychological factors that drive performance and innovation. That's where we get into trouble.

Radio, at its heart, is a *people business.* And yet, we've allowed it to become too impersonal. Too corporate. Too cold. We've forgotten that our greatest asset walks in and out of the building every day.

When leadership becomes detached, teams suffer. Morale dips. Communication fractures. Creativity dries up. And yes, talent walks.

But when leaders show up—really show up—they set the tone for everyone else. They model the values they want their team to embrace. They create an atmosphere of respect, responsibility, and resilience. They *flip the format on fear.*

As a licensed psychotherapist and a former broadcaster, I know that fear is a quiet killer in any organization. It undermines confidence, silences innovation, and breeds toxicity. That's why leaders must be brave enough to be vulnerable, strong enough to be honest, and present enough to listen.

If you're in a leadership role in radio—or in any business—ask yourself:

- Do my team members feel seen and heard?
- Have I built a culture of trust?
- Am I modeling the behavior I want from others?

If you can't answer yes to these questions, it's time to recalibrate. It's time to step up. To walk the talk. To flip the format on fear and lead like you mean it.

Because in the end, great leaders don't just manage people—they *inspire* them. And in radio, that inspiration can travel farther than any signal.

📻 Mike McVay's Insider Perspective; Leaders who mentored me and taught me to be a responsible leader.

Observing others is a great way to learn leadership. Both the good and bad sides of leadership. The first couple leaders I had while working part-time in radio spent little time with me, and why should they? I was a kid going to school who worked a few hours on the weekend. The mentorship I received in that stage of my career came from air talent who shared their experiences and offered suggestions on how I might improve. They're the reason that I continue to spend time mentoring others. Their advice, caring, and interest in my improvement, was truly beneficial to me.

The owner and General Manager of the radio station I programmed and where I hosted mornings in Wheeling, W.Va. was a true showman. He had worked at carnivals, he booked and managed acts, he was a lifelong broadcaster, and he took me under his wing. His wife was the receptionist who doubled as a "Secretary" (a job title from the 70s) and she taught me business. She'd say "In the morning, you need to be prepared to tell me what you need me to focus on for the day. Otherwise, we get nothing done."

He'd use analogies to teach me. I remember once he told me the story of a country artist he was hiring to perform a show at Jamboree USA. He asked the artist how long his set was. The singer said, "30 minutes." He said "How much of it is really good? Your best stuff." The artist said, "15 minutes." He told the artist "Just give me the best 15 minutes and I'll pay you for 30." I got the message. Do my best on the air, even if it means talking less.

The managers who made themselves accessible to me got the most out of me. The ones that engaged in dialogue and collaboration inspired loyalty and dedication. Leaders who made me feel as if I was on their level motivated me to work harder for them as I felt like we were in the same boat. One of us wasn't on shore with the other yelling "Row." Those who approached management in a Lords & Serfs type of structure usually failed despite opportunities to succeed even when accomplishment was within their reach.

It's Not About Control—It's About Care

Responsibility doesn't mean micromanagement. In fact, control freaks rarely empower their teams. But responsible leaders provide frameworks, set standards, and trust their people to rise to the occasion.

If someone fails, it's not a finger-pointing session. It's a conversation: *"What didn't work? How can we support you?"*

Leadership means creating a culture where responsibility is shared—not feared.

✅ WORKSHEET: Leadership Ownership Audit
Reflection Questions:

- When have I taken responsibility for something that wasn't technically "my job"? What happened?
- How do I respond when someone on my team fails?
- Where am I currently avoiding ownership out of fear?

Action Steps:

- Identify one daily task where you can lead by example.
- Choose a team member and acknowledge something they've taken responsibility for this week.
- Begin a "Wins + Lessons" journal: Track small moments of responsibility and what they taught you.

📢 Final Thoughts: Respect Starts with Responsibility

When you show up with responsibility—consistently, calmly, and compassionately—you create a ripple effect that transforms culture.

You're not flipping the format to get attention. You're doing it to build trust, foster resilience, and set a new standard for leadership in your industry.

Let's be honest—responsibility isn't always fun. But it is always respected.

Now go out there, lead with integrity, and flip the format on fear— one responsible choice at a time.

CHAPTER 9

The Art of Resilience in a Changing Industry

W.K.R.P. Framework: Resilience

Resilience Is Not Optional Anymore

In radio—as in life—change is constant. But in recent years, the pace of change has become relentless. Stations close, formats flip, ownership changes, technology evolves, and entire careers pivot in the blink of an eye.

This isn't fearmongering. This is our reality. And in that reality, resilience is no longer just a nice-to-have trait. It's a must-have mindset.

The most successful broadcasters aren't the ones who cling to old models or resist the tide. They are the ones who *adapt with intention*. They are resilient, responsible, and respectful in the face of uncertainty—and they grow stronger with every challenge.

When Everything Changed for Me

There was a moment—years ago—when I thought my career was over. My body said *stop*, and my heart nearly did.

It was during this time, recovering from heart failure and grappling with an uncertain future, that I realized: this wasn't the end. It was an opportunity to rebuild with intention.

I had a background in radio. I had experience in business. But now, I had something else: **a new perspective**. I went back to school to become a therapist. I leaned into what I already knew—*how to communicate, how to connect, and how to pivot.*

That experience became my personal case study in resilience. I didn't bounce *back*. I bounced *forward*.

And so can you.

There's No "Back to Normal"—And That's a Good Thing

Normal is a setting on the clothes dryer.

There are a few things we can all agree on — even if we've never met. We are living in a time of tremendous stress and uncertainty. Most of us are afraid. And no matter where you are in the world or what business you're in, we are all affected by this pandemic.

The question of the day, though, seems to be, "When do we get back to normal?"

Can I just say — *normal doesn't exist anymore.* That ship has sailed. In fact, I'd argue that the world we knew pre-pandemic wasn't all that normal to begin with.

There was a lot of dysfunction in that "normal." Unreasonable expectations. Lack of balance. Commuting burnout. Mental health stigma. A culture of burnout — with an unhealthy dose of shame for needing to slow down.

And that's just at work.

Now that so many things have been turned upside-down, it's time to flip the format.

This is our moment to rethink how we do things. In radio. In business. In relationships. And especially — in leadership.

You've probably heard the phrase "a new normal" a dozen times already. And maybe you're already sick of it. I am too.

But let's not confuse "new normal" with "worse."

What if this disruption gives us permission to reimagine?

What if you don't "go back to work" — but instead return with purpose?

What if your team becomes more productive — because they're less stressed, less afraid, and feel more valued?

What if this season of social distancing has actually created opportunities for deeper human connection?

And what if — after everything — you come out of this crisis with more clarity, more confidence, and more courage?

As a mental health professional, broadcaster, and business consultant — I want to say: this isn't just wishful thinking. It's possible. But it won't happen by accident.

The biggest shift will need to happen inside each of us.

This isn't about bouncing back. It's about bouncing forward. Resilience isn't about returning to where you were — it's about rising stronger than before.

You've probably been running on autopilot for years. We all have.

The same routines. The same goals. The same stress.

Well, now the autopilot's been turned off. We're forced to take the wheel.

That might be scary — but it's also empowering.

So instead of focusing on "getting back to normal," I invite you to reflect on this instead:

- What have you learned during this time that you want to carry forward?
- What habits or routines were actually hurting you — that you now have permission to leave behind?
- Who are you — when the distractions and noise are gone?
- What values do you want to lead with — at home, at work, and in your community?

This is your invitation to rewrite your script.

I've been in broadcasting long enough to know that sometimes, the best thing you can do for a tired format is flip it.

New music. New voices. A new perspective.

That's what I want to offer you. Not a return to what was — but a path to what's next.

If you're a leader in any capacity — at home, in your company, on your team — now is the time to lead with empathy, clarity, and courage. That means being human first. That means listening more. That means making space for grief, growth, and gratitude — all at once.

And it means you go first. You can't lead anyone else where you haven't gone yourself.

I believe we are on the edge of something transformational. But you have to choose to participate.

Don't go back. Go forward.

It's not about "normal."

It's about being *better* than before.

Apple a Day: Bounce Forward, Not Just Back

"Resilience isn't about pretending things are fine—it's about finding strength even when they're not."

Emotional elasticity—how to stretch without snapping. That's the heart of resilience.

Think about your own bounce-back moments. What helped you get through them?

- A supportive mentor?
- A moment of clarity?
- A shift in routine?

Now consider this: What if resilience was like a muscle you could train?

Start small:

- Identify a daily stressor.
- Choose a healthier response.
- Celebrate the win.

Do it again tomorrow.

And the next day.

Pretty soon, you've built the habit of hope.

Mike McVay's Insider Insight - The 3WE Story - Mobile, Alabama - Back to CLE

Flipping the Format led to a career flip for me and a sidetrack that had short term negatives with long term positives. WWWE/WDOK are AM/FM stations in Cleveland, Ohio. I was hired to program WWWE (3WE) and serve as Operations Manager of both stations. WDOK was Easy Listening and soon to change format to Soft AC. 3WE was an MOR (Standards like John Denver and Neil Diamond) with personalities. The plan when I joined was to conduct a research project and, if supported by the research, find a new format for 3WE.

The study results supported changing the station's format to News/Talk. The station already had a 7:00pm-12:00am nightly sports talk program, and it was the flagship for the Cleveland Indians baseball. We made our plans. Put together logos, marketing suggestions, and were planning to keep the existing talent, but realigning their show times.

We made the presentation to station ownership, which was a large corporation. They sat through the research, asked the researcher to "give us the room", and then proceeded to tell the General Manager and me that they intended for the station to change formats to Country. Country music on an AM station at 1100 on the dial. Failure was on the horizon.

It was apparent to me that the job I had taken six months earlier was about to go in a very wrong direction. They asked me if I wanted to stay on and program country music on a 50,000-watt AM in a market that had an FM country station and another AM country station in it. We'd be the third station doing country music in a time when music formats were moving from AM to FM. I said no, almost immediately. They asked me to give it more thought. I gave it another week and then validated my earlier negative response. My advice is to never quit without another job, which is what I'd just done. Were it not for luck, things could have turned out badly.

Prior to me taking the job in Cleveland, I had been in conversation with a legendary owner named Bernie Dittman, who had made famous WABB AM/FM in Mobile, Alabama. I'd done a side project for Bernie. He wanted me to come to work for him, but instead I took the position in Cleveland. My title was Station Manager, but I was working under a General Manager, and so the job at 3WE was really that of Operations Manager/Program Director. When Bernie heard that I'd resigned from Cleveland, he called me and said, "If you want to be a General Manager, come here and I'll teach you how to manage and run a radio station." I took the job. My wife and our 2-year-old daughter were moving in under a year to Mobile, Alabama.

When asked, my wife says "Mobile is a cute city. It's very pretty." I usually say, "It was the longest year of my life." Only because I never felt like I fit into the lifestyle of the deep south in the early 80s. It was a great work experience, though. Bernie showed me the ropes, taught me sales and collections, pushed me to learn every part of the operation, and taught me discipline. I don't mean that he disciplined me. He taught me to be the first in and the last out. To never ask someone to do something that you wouldn't do yourself, and he taught me the value of people. He was a tough mentor, but a good mentor. We lost him far too soon.

The year I spent in Mobile, learning to manage and be deeply involved in sales, enabled me to return to Cleveland and become the General Manager of two stations. Larry "JB" Robinson was a successful jeweler who owned JB Robinson Jewelers throughout the Midwest. He had 72 stores when I first went to work for him. He voiced his own commercials and that's what lit the fuse for him to buy stations in his hometown. We flipped the format on a Rock FM to Oldies Based AC and renamed M105 to WMJI/Majic 105.7fm. The station debuted #1 Adults 25-54. The other station was WBBG-AM, and it featured Music of Your Life. That was a format of music from the 40s, 50s, and 60s. It was already #1 12+ when I arrived.

Working with Larry Robinson, Larry Pollock (the President of the jewelry business), and Tom Embrescia (the previous owner) gave me experience beyond what you'd learn in an MBA program. In reality, Larry Robinson had been a professor at Harvard teaching Business Administration when his father died, and he had to return to Cleveland to run the jewelry stores. Larry Pollock was well educated and a highly successful retailer who later in his career ran Kay Jewelers. Tom continued in radio as an owner/operator after he sold to Robinson. He was an early investor and founding partner in McVay Media. He hired me to consult him in St. Louis, Milwaukee and Indianapolis.

When the format was literally flipped at 1100 AM to Country (which lasted for under two years) it would have been easy for me to be passive aggressive and stay in the position or leave and complain in a "woe is me" fashion, but instead I chose to take advantage of the situation and learn for the future. While we all have a "Use By" date in our lives, our careers need not. It's like finding the end of the internet. If you're going to continue to be a part of society, an industry, a business, why wouldn't you make the best of it? We're here. Let's enjoy the ride.

Action Worksheet: Resilience Reset

☑ **Step 1:** Write down one recent professional or personal setback.

☑ **Step 2:** Identify one thing it taught you.

☑ **Step 3:** Choose one action you can take this week to move forward.

☑ **Step 4:** Commit to checking in on your progress in 7 days.

Final Thoughts: Format Flips Start Within

Resilience doesn't just happen. It's practiced. It's built. It's chosen.

In this ever-evolving industry, your ability to recover and reframe is your *greatest asset.* Not just as a broadcaster—but as a leader, a colleague, and a human being.

Change is coming. Don't fear it. *Flip the format.*

And remember: You've been Licensed2BBadass all along.

PART 4

P — Positive Psychology

Chapters 10 – 12

CHAPTER 10

Positive Psychology for Broadcasters

W.K.R.P. Framework: P — Positive Psychology

Why Positive Leadership Creates Stronger Teams

Leadership is more than making decisions—it's about shaping the emotional climate of your station. And in a high-pressure, fast-changing industry like radio, how a leader shows up can either uplift or unravel the entire team.

 In a business built on creativity, timing, and relationships, resilience becomes a performance tool—and it starts at the top.

Let's explore why positive leadership builds resilient, successful teams—and how you can develop those skills, no matter your title.

The Impact of Leadership Energy

Your leadership energy is contagious. Whether you're in the corner office or working the overnight shift, how you show up affects others. Positive leaders:

- Foster trust, confidence, and collaboration
- Build psychological safety and reduce stress
- Inspire innovation and risk-taking

Fear-based leadership does the opposite:

- Increases anxiety and burnout

- Shuts down creativity and communication
- Drives high turnover and low morale

The good news? You don't have to be born a leader to become one. Positive leadership is a mindset, a skillset, and a choice.

The Leadership Shift That Changed Everything

There was a time in my own leadership journey when I focused more on performance than people. I thought high expectations would automatically lead to high results. But something was missing.

I wasn't supporting the emotional energy of my team.

I learned the hard way that excellence without empathy leads to exhaustion. So, I flipped the format. I led with intention, not just expectations. I started recognizing wins, creating space for feedback, and supporting growth—not just output.

The transformation in my teams was immediate. Engagement rose. Innovation returned. And our results didn't just improve—they became more sustainable.

That was the moment I became a Licensed2BBadass leader.

The Science of Positive Leadership

Leadership is not about being "nice"—it's about being intentional.

Psychological research confirms:

- Employees who feel valued are 50% more productive.
- Teams with positive cultures are 3x more creative and engaged.

- Resilient leaders experience lower turnover and higher trust.

And emotional intelligence (EQ) plays a massive role. EQ is the ability to recognize, regulate, and respond to emotions—yours and others'. It's more important than IQ for leadership effectiveness.

Developing a Powerful Leadership Presence

Four decades is a long time to spend in one industry. I've had a front-row seat to the evolution of radio and a backstage pass to the emotional toll it can take. I talk to a lot of people in radio, specifically on the topic of stress, anxiety, depression and how to get more out of their teams.

There was a time when I believed more structure, more rules, and more control were the answers. But as the burnout mounted and innovation stalled, I realized that fear was driving too many decisions—from the boardroom to the breakroom. The biggest problem in radio is that people are afraid to take a risk, for fear of failing.

So, I began to pivot. I applied my psychological training and my leadership experience to shift the energy. I coached my team differently. I opened up space for vulnerability and creativity. I stopped pretending I had all the answers and started asking better questions.

That shift created deeper engagement. People felt seen. They contributed more. They took risks and collaborated with courage. And guess what? Performance improved too.

Leadership presence isn't about perfection. It's about presence. Being aware, being human, and being intentional with your influence.

Educating myself 'after-the-fact' has really been a benefit. I returned to school to get a degree in psychology and formal training in therapy. That decision changed everything for me. I now have case studies, education, and research to back up what I know intuitively through decades of lived experience. I've become a better leader because I've become a better learner.

That's the growth mindset in action. And it's available to anyone willing to evolve. You don't need a license to lead—but you do need a willingness to grow.

These fears—when unaddressed—show up in leadership. They lead to control instead of collaboration. Silence instead of strategy. The antidote? Positive leadership is built on courage, compassion, and connection.

Key Traits of Positive Leaders

- **Clarity Over Chaos**
    - Great leaders provide certainty in uncertain times.
    - Set clear expectations
    - Communicate consistently
    - Follow through on your word
    - ✅ Clarity reduces anxiety and builds trust.
- **Support Over Sabotage**
    - Micromanaging kills motivation. Positive leaders coach, encourage, and empower.

- Offer feedback that fuels, not flattens
- Acknowledge effort, not just outcomes
- Ask: "How can I support you?"
- **Psychological Safety Over Fear**
  - When people feel safe, they contribute more.
  - Normalize mistakes as learning opportunities
  - Encourage open dialogue
  - Celebrate courage, not just competence

One producer I worked with had brilliant ideas—but kept them to herself because the room didn't feel safe. Once leadership shifted, her creativity helped launch one of the station's most successful promotions.

- **Growth Over Ego**
  - Positive leaders are lifelong learners.
  - Read. Study. Seek mentors.
  - Ask for feedback.
  - Stay curious—not controlling.

That's the growth mindset in action.

Sometimes I Need a Pep Talk

There are days I just don't have the energy. Days when the usual tools don't work and the positive mindset feels miles away.

In those moments, I give myself a pep talk.

I remind myself of who I am, what I've done, and what I'm still capable of. It's not about toxic positivity. It's about resetting.

I've recorded voice memos for myself in the past, literally talking myself through a funk. "Hey, Kelly. You're tired. That's okay. But remember what you've overcome. Remember who's watching. Remember why you started."

Sometimes, I even listen to my own podcast to hear the words I've told others. Turns out, I needed them too.

That's the thing about positive psychology—it's not about always feeling good. It's about having tools for when you don't.

Apple A Day: Smile and the World Smiles with You

You can shift a room with a smile. It's not magic; it's science. Smiling releases endorphins—your brain's natural mood boosters. And they're contagious.

I remember walking into a meeting where the energy was low. Tension was thick. I made it a point to smile, genuinely, at each person I greeted. By the end of the meeting, things felt different. Lighter. More hopeful.

Positive energy doesn't mean ignoring reality. It means influencing it.

Try this: For one day, smile at every person you encounter. Not a fake one. A real one. See what happens.

Badass leaders know that optimism is a discipline. And that smile? It's your first tool.

Positive Psychology for Broadcasters

Broadcasting is high-pressure, high-reward, and highly emotional. Positive psychology offers powerful tools for thriving in that environment.

1. Gratitude resets the brain.

2. Mindset reframes the moment.

3. Strengths-based focus builds confidence.

Start meetings by sharing what went well. Ask your team what they're proud of. Use affirmations. Celebrate the small wins.

And most importantly, lead by example.

If you want to flip the format on fear, you have to broadcast courage, connection, and compassion—loud and clear.

Mike McVay's Insider Insight - Positive Cultures VS Ego Centered Leadership

There is a need for a healthy dose of ego in our DNA, but it shouldn't be overwhelming. Most of us have seen leaders that follow the Bull in A China Shop management style. They're aggressive, pushy, demanding, and push directives without explanation. Ego centric leaders care more about how they look trying to succeed than they do in actually succeeding.

My long-held belief is that leaders who are brash and bullying are likely lacking in confidence, unsure of the pathway to success, and quite possibly in fear of losing their job. Those who know me well know that I am a huge fan of my hometown Pittsburgh Steelers.

Legendary Steelers former head coach Chuck Knoll once said, "Pressure is when you don't know what you're doing."

Positive cultures come when there's a clearly stated "cause", open dialogue, clear direction, explanation of the "Why" and guidance regarding the "How." Presentation of what accomplishment looks like. If you don't know what you're doing something, then how do you even know if you're doing it the right way? Positive cultures have clear guidelines and benchmarks to signal where you are on the journey. Positive cultures have a destination in mind. An Australian counterpart of mine likes to say, "If you don't know where you're going, then any road will take you there."

Leadership is telling your team that you're going to hike to the mountain top, explaining why you're making the hike, what happens when you arrive at the peak, and encouraging them to follow you.

Leadership Toolkit: How to Practice Positive Leadership

☑ **Conduct a Positivity Inventory:** What's going well? Share it with your team. Then do more of it.

☑ **Try a Small-Scale Change:** Pilot one new method or practice in a single department. Track results. Refine and repeat.

☑ **Recognize Contributions:** Praise publicly, correct privately. Make appreciation part of your leadership brand.

☑ **Invite Input:** Ask your team what they need. Give them voice and agency.

☑ **Model Self-Care:** If you're burnt out, your team will be too. Walk the walk.

Actionable Worksheet: Your Positive Leadership Plan
Step 1: Leadership Check-In

What is one belief you have about leadership that might need updating?

Step 2: Identify a Strength

Where do you naturally lead well—clarity, empathy, support?

Step 3: Spot a Growth Opportunity

What part of your leadership needs development?

Step 4: Take a Bold Action

Choose one way to lead more positively this week. Track the outcome.

Final Thoughts: You Set the Tone

Every team reflects its leadership. That's not pressure—it's power.

📻 In radio, you're in the business of influencing people. As a leader, your greatest influence begins inside your own station. When you model resilience, positivity, and progress, your team will echo it.

And when you lead with authenticity and intention? You become the kind of leader people want to follow.

You're already Licensed2BBadass. Now lead like it.

CHAPTER 11

The Future of Radio and Adapting to Change

W.K.R.P. Framework: P — Positive Psychology

Rewiring Begins Where Fear Used to Live

There's a reason why this chapter follows the one on burnout. Because when we reach the edge—when fear, exhaustion, and doubt take hold—it's not just our schedule that needs reworking. It's our mindset.

Flipping the format on fear isn't just a clever title. It's a daily, gritty, honest process of retraining your brain to respond differently. Fear used to run the show. But it doesn't have to forever.

Let's start with the science—and then we'll move into stories.

Neuroplasticity: The Brain's Greatest Feature

Your brain is neuroplastic, which means it can rewire itself through new thoughts, habits, and emotional responses. That's not just psychology—it's biology.

In stressful industries like radio, fear often becomes the default setting:

- Fear of sounding stupid
- Fear of being replaced
- Fear of losing relevance

These aren't just emotional experiences. They're neurological patterns. But the good news is: you can flip the signal.

The brain follows the mind. And the mind can be trained to expect growth instead of collapse, curiosity instead of shame, creativity instead of comparison.

Personal Story: My Mind Didn't Know I Was Strong—Until I Proved It

When I was diagnosed with congestive heart failure, my confidence and energy collapsed. The physical symptoms were brutal—but what really haunted me was the mental spiral:

"Who am I if I can't work? What if I never bounce back?"

I started journaling—not because I was feeling hopeful, but because I wasn't. I began writing three things I was grateful for. I visualized what healing might look like, even when I didn't believe it.

With every small act of commitment—one class, one assignment, one reflection—I built proof for my brain.

That's how neuroplasticity works. Every moment of courage rewires your identity.

Fear and Love Can't Occupy the Same Frequency

One of the most powerful lessons I teach clients is this: there are only two emotional signals—fear and love.

And your brain cannot transmit both at the same time.

- Fear restricts. Love expands.
- Fear says, "You'll fail."

- Love says, "Let's try."
- Fear says, "You're too old."
- Love says, "You're still growing."

When you catch yourself spiraling in fear, pause and ask: What would this thought sound like if it came from love instead of fear?

That single shift can change your entire emotional frequency.

Emotional Projection and Self-Awareness

During coaching sessions with executives and on-air talent, I've seen it time and time again: conflict that isn't about the project or task—it's about unprocessed fear.

Maybe you're projecting old rejection onto your PD. Or you're assuming your boss doubts you because you doubt yourself. Fear loves to hijack reality.

When I say that personal and professional growth go hand in hand, this is what I mean. You can't build creative, confident teams if the individuals haven't learned to regulate their own fears.

Tune Your Brain Like a Station

Think of your brain like a radio tower. If you keep tuning into static, doubt, or rage, that's what you're going to hear. But you can choose a different signal.

You can broadcast:

- Peace over panic
- Curiosity over perfection
- Belief over burnout

And the more you choose it, the clearer that frequency becomes.

Why Adaptability is the New Superpower

The only constant in radio—and life—is change. Technology shifts. Formats evolve. Platforms expand. But one thing remains: the need for human connection. In radio, that connection happens through sound, story, and spontaneity.

To thrive in the future of broadcasting, we must reframe change not as a threat, but as an invitation to evolve.

Let's explore how adaptability, optimism, and identity alignment allow radio professionals to not just survive change—but lead it.

The Myth of Radio's Demise

Radio has been declared dead more times than we can count:

- "AM is dying."
- "FM is obsolete."
- "Streaming is king."

And yet—radio persists. Why?

Because it adapts.

From vinyl to voice assistants, the soul of radio—its authenticity and intimacy—continues to find new formats. Positive psychology tells us that optimism fuels perseverance. It's not about denying change; it's about engaging with it.

Perception vs. Reality

I really don't know how people perceive me. Not until somebody spells it out for me, and truthfully, people's "perception" of who and what they think of me isn't always an accurate description of what and who I am.

Social media alters people's perception of others. One can create a "persona" on Facebook, Twitter, LinkedIn and all the other social networks and "be" whomever they choose to be.

Who are you?

What message do you put out into the world?

What if the message that is perceived isn't the message you intended?

Here's another fun story about my Victorville radio experiences.

Papa Was A Rolling Stone

Changing the format of a radio station is often a necessity due to increased competition, the marketplace shifting, the need for something fresh, new ownership, or just the desire to go in a different direction based on the needs of the community. Businesses of all kinds will change their model, offer new services, and update their image. Radio is really no different.

There came a summer where we planned to change our format from a soft music format (yawn!) to an "Oldies" station. The market had changed, and we needed a format we could "own." Oldies felt like our roots, so we decided to head back to the beginning.

Let's remember: this was a family-owned radio station. We made our own decisions and had a lot of fun brainstorming ideas. As the ideas flowed—it was decided that to garner attention to the impending format change, we'd play just **one song in a loop for 24 hours**. That would be enough time for listeners to sense a change coming, and it gave us time to notify advertisers.

We chose "Papa Was a Rolling Stone" by The Temptations. The intro was two minutes long, and the lyrics mentioned 'the third of September,' which happened to be the exact date of the format flip. We couldn't have orchestrated it better.

So, on **September 2nd**, the station began looping "Papa Was a Rolling Stone." After just 10–15 minutes, the phones rang off the hook. Listeners wanted to know what the heck was going on.

Perception Becomes Reality

Our staff was told to say nothing. We wanted anticipation. But one of our staffers, caught off guard, jokingly told a caller, *"One of our DJs went nuts and locked himself in the studio and now he's playing this song over and over again!"*

That one comment snowballed.

Listeners thought the DJ was **suicidal** or **holding us hostage**. The phones kept ringing. We tried to reassure people, but they were calling 911, church pastors, the local paper—even a TV station in Los Angeles.

We had pastors come by. Police dropped in. A news team reached out. Every visitor we told the truth to was sworn to secrecy. This was still a business strategy.

The **interest and publicity** we got was priceless.

But the perception was: there was a crisis at the station.

Meanwhile—we were having a blast.

Once the official announcement was made and Oldies began to play, the local paper ran the story front page. Listeners loved the music—but many were mad that we'd worried them.

We didn't intend to send the wrong message. It just happened.

That's what perception does—it can mask reality.

Be Mindful of the Message You Put into the World

You don't control how others perceive you. And sometimes, perception carries more weight than intent.

The "crazy DJ" stunt became one of the **most talked-about promotions** in our station's history. It wasn't what we planned—but it worked.

The lesson? Be mindful of what people might **perceive** about you. And if they misunderstand—try not to take it personally. Just adapt, respond with integrity, and keep going.

Apple A Day

Being adaptable means being able to adjust to new conditions. It means being flexible, open to change, and resilient when things don't go according to plan.

Sometimes, we resist change because we're comfortable. But growth never happens in the comfort zone. Being adaptable allows you to thrive in uncertain situations, to take risks, and to grow.

So, the next time things don't go as planned, instead of getting frustrated or stuck, remind yourself: I am adaptable. I am flexible. I will adjust and move forward.

Adaptability is not a weakness, it's a strength. Be adaptable. Be BADASS.

Radio is Not Dead—It's Evolving

I was once talking to a Program Director about the evolution of formats. He lamented that even though their format and presentation were working, their challenge was that everything had changed.

"I used to ask, 'What do we play?' Now I ask, 'How do we stay alive? How do we stay relevant?'"

That was a profound moment. Formats are not only evolving; they are required to evolve. We're not just competing with other radio stations, we're competing with streaming audio, YouTube, TV, podcasts, and social media. Yet even amid all of that competition, our listeners are still listening to the radio. The delivery of our content has changed, but the connection we have with our listeners is still very real.

What Hasn't Changed? The Human Voice.

It still connects. And while the delivery method may have changed—smart speakers, Spotify, apps, or streaming—it's still about the voice that brings comfort, news, companionship, and local flavor.

You are no longer "just" a DJ, talk host, or news anchor—you're the bridge. The connector. You are the real human being among algorithm-generated playlists and AI-generated news summaries. You're the live voice in a world full of canned content. That hasn't changed—and that's our superpower.

Radio's Greatest Challenge is Evolution

It's not death. It's adaptation. Hybrid formats, localized content, new delivery methods, and smarter audience engagement are the future. But the heartbeat of radio is still the human voice and the relationships we've built with our audiences.

Radio is not dead. It's evolving. And that's a good thing.

Mike McVay's Insider Insight

Because of the growth and expansion of media, continually evolving and changing, legacy media (Radio, Television, Satellite Radio, Theatres, Movies on Demand) is seeing erosion as is new media (podcasting, streaming, social media), due to the boundaries that time puts upon us. We have 24 hours in a day. It doesn't matter how many platforms are added, the time in a day remains the same. We are seeing the first wave of DSP's (streamers) lose subscribers. SiriusXM has been on a reinvention journey since the pandemic as they try to compete with Spotify.

When Radio and TV were all there was, it was easy. A friend of mine talks about when in the late 60s and early 70s they had a 30 share of ratings in their market. I "gig" him by stating that he should've had a 50 share because there were only two Top 40 stations. We'll never see those days again, but that doesn't mean that there won't be dominant radio stations and that certainly doesn't mean that radio isn't relevant today. The DSP's wish that they had radio's distribution and reach. There's a reason why they shield their audience numbers. They aren't what they want you to believe that they are, and they talk about impressions and not cume or time spent listening.

That's not to diminish the power of streaming. It is a great distribution platform, and smart broadcasters are streaming their stations. The reality of radio today is that it must be over the air, online, on smart speakers, on demand via apps, and using podcasting to expand its' reach.

Radio must be ubiquitous.

Worksheet: Adapt Your Mindset

☑ Step 1: Identify one area of your professional life that's changing right now.

☑ Step 2: Ask yourself—am I resisting or responding?

☑ Step 3: Reframe the situation using positive language.

☑ Step 4: Make one adaptable action plan this week to move forward with confidence.

Final Thoughts: You're Already Evolving

Adaptability isn't just about survival—it's about thriving. The industry is changing, and so are you. Whether you're flipping a format, reinventing a show, or redefining your personal brand, every shift is an opportunity.

Don't fear the evolution. **Be the one who leads it.**

CHAPTER 12

Becoming the Leader You Were Meant to Be

W.K.R.P. Framework: P — Positive Psychology

Leadership Isn't a Title—It's a Decision

Some people wait for the promotion. Others wait to be noticed. But great leaders don't wait—they lead.

Leadership is not a title you earn from someone else—it's an identity you choose. It begins with mindset, grows with experience, and flourishes with authenticity.

In my journey through the radio industry—and in my work as a psychotherapist and leadership coach—I've seen the full spectrum. I've worked with managers who ruled with fear and burned-out entire teams. And I've partnered with quiet professionals who led with calm strength, transforming stations and culture from the inside out.

Becoming the leader, you were meant to be means starting with what's already inside of you.

My Radio Roots: Leadership Without a Nameplate

I didn't become a leader because someone handed me a business card that said so. I became one because I learned the power of showing up.

In the early days at KVVQ-FM in Victorville, we were a family-run operation. There was no hierarchy to climb—there was only work to be done. I did traffic, billing, engineering, promotions, and yes—even janitorial tasks.

One day, a major-market jock joined our team. He didn't give me the time of day—until the automation system went down. I knew how to fix it. I did. And from that day forward, he saw me differently.

That experience taught me: respect is earned by action, not assumed through status.

Leading Through Emotional Intelligence

Emotional intelligence (EQ) is one of the most critical indicators of leadership success. It allows you to regulate your own emotions, interpret the emotional states of others, and foster motivation rather than fear. EQ-based leadership fosters trust, cultivates healthy communication, and minimizes unnecessary conflict.

Many assume that leadership is about experience or charisma—but in truth, EQ often matters more than IQ. A leader who understands emotional nuance can inspire more engagement and build teams that thrive under pressure.

📌 **Tip:** When conflict arises, ask: "What fear might be driving this behavior?" Then lead with empathy, not ego.

My Leadership Style: A Democratic Approach

During graduate school, I discovered a term that matched how I had led all along—democratic leadership.

"A democratic leader delegates authority to others, encourages participation, relies on subordinates' knowledge for completion of tasks, and depends on subordinate respect for influence."

That was me. I never chased leadership for power or control. My path wasn't about dominance—it was about contribution, collaboration, and understanding human behavior. That's what makes a team thrive.

Through formal study and real-life experience, I learned how people behave individually and in groups—and I learned how to help them flourish.

The Five Core Traits of a True Leader

- **Self-Awareness: Know Thyself First**
  - You cannot lead others well if you don't understand your own emotional triggers, strengths, and weaknesses.
- **Leaders with self-awareness:**
  - Know their limits and communicate them.
  - Recognize emotional patterns and regulate their responses.
  - Accept feedback without defensiveness.

☁ **Action:** Journal your emotional triggers during high-stress moments. What causes frustration? What thoughts follow?

- **Resilience: The Engine of Sustainable Leadership**
  - Resilient leaders don't avoid failure—they expect it. But they don't fear it.

- When I experienced a health crisis, it halted everything. My leadership identity took a hit. But through therapy, writing, and teaching, I redefined my purpose.

Resilience isn't something you're born with—it's something you practice. Over and over. It's in the moments when you feel like giving up—but don't. It's in the silent strength you summon when everything feels uncertain. The more you practice it, the more natural it becomes. And eventually, resilience isn't just what you do—it's who you are."

- **Vision: Seeing Beyond the Studio Walls**
  - Great leaders look beyond deadlines and current ratings—they imagine what's possible.
  - Visionary leaders:
1. Ask, "What will this team need six months from now?"
2. Build culture intentionally, not reactively.
3. Inspire others by painting a picture of the future.

🖋 **Action:** Write your 12-month leadership vision. What kind of environment are you creating?

1. Influence: Leading Without Authority

Real leaders don't need a title to make an impact. Some of the most influential people I've met never had "manager" in their job description. But they moved people. They inspired change.

Influence is built through:

1. Trust

2. Consistency

3. Integrity

⟳ **Action:** Reflect on someone who influenced you without authority. What did they model that you can adopt?

1. Commitment to Growth: Be the Leader Who Learns

I'm a learner. It's one of my top strengths. When I coach or teach, I research the latest trends. I learn from my students. I grow from the experience.

Great leaders:

1. Read, listen, attend workshops.

2. Seek mentorship and constructive feedback.

3. Apply what they learn, consistently.

▤ **Action:** What leadership lesson have you learned in the last 30 days? How will you use it?

From Management to Mentorship

You don't need to control people—you need to care about them.

When I teach market managers and program directors, I remind them: You are not just managing output. You are shaping careers, inspiring confidence, and setting the emotional temperature of your workplace.

Open yourself up to your team. Ask about their goals. Invite their ideas. Share your own radio story—the highs, the setbacks, the ridiculous promos and off-air pranks. Stories breed connection.

When people feel seen, they show up stronger.

Real Leaders Elevate Others

Leadership isn't micromanaging—it's microphone sharing.

I interviewed a program director who dramatically improved team performance by shifting from top-down directives to inclusive collaboration.

Instead of commanding every aspect of production, he began his team meetings with a single question: "What do YOU think?"

"That one shift made our team unstoppable," he said. "They started offering ideas before I even asked. I saw engagement go through the roof. The work became a true collaboration—not just execution."

This transformation didn't just increase morale—it lifted ratings. The PD became a model of how trust, humility, and curiosity are better leadership tools than control or ego.

We also spotlighted how sharing the mic—figuratively and literally—gave younger talent a chance to grow and shine. One weekend board-op eventually became the host of her own afternoon drive show—all because her input was valued and her ideas were heard.

True leadership in radio doesn't mean dominating every broadcast—it means building a culture where every voice matters.

Mike McVay's Insider Insight

My approach to leadership starts with The Golden Rule. It's Biblical. "Do unto others as you would like to be done unto you." Lead like you like to be led. That's at the core of how I've led from the beginning. Perhaps because I had interest in becoming a theology student, but I suspect it is more so because of those who were leaders in my early days of media. I watched, paid attention, and learned by example.

Because of my approach to organization, structure is important to me. I need and want structure that allows routine to become second nature. Having a strong organized foundation allows for easy execution, and that allows for creativity. It may be counterintuitive, but what enables creativity is "getting the work out of the way so you can focus on playtime." Think about it. If I execute those tasks that need to be handled, and they're "out of the way" it then allows me to clear my brain and be creative. Discipline is at the root of creativity. Allowing creatives to address their jobs, completing tasks, should lead to playtime.

A system that I've long used centered at one time on physical files. Today those files are on my laptop and connected to my phone. Seven files; Active, one for each day Monday-Friday, and Future. I place in the Active file the things I am working on right now. Each daily file is something I want to work on as the week goes on, but those items can be moved back a day or two as the week progresses. Priorities do change. The file marked Future is exactly that. Could be for next week or a couple weeks down the road. Things that are scheduled for down the road go onto my calendar, versus in a file, so that when they pop up they move into a Daily or Active file.

The other thing I do is make lists. I have two small note pads that I keep with me. One has the heading of the day (i.e. Monday, etcetera) and the other says "To Do." The one titled with a day name is a duplicate of my phone calendar and notes to myself as reminders. The "To Do" are not priorities, but I don't want to forget about those tasks. It is a duplication of effort, but it also keeps these tasks top of mind for me.

Being organized enables me to lead by compartmentalizing tasks and focusing on the greater initiatives that are to be accomplished. That foundation allows me to lead with clarity and give my team members the focus necessary to direct them. I always share what the objective is, how I believe we can accomplish it, what actions are necessary to do so, and who is assigned to do what. A deadline for accomplishment is always given, too. Then the most important part of leadership, allowing for collaboration, suggestions, and recommendations. My belief is that a leader always has the right to say "No." So, why not consider other approaches to a project.

📝 Actionable Worksheet: Define Your Leadership Path
✓ Step 1: Identify Your Strengths

List 3 things people often praise you for.

✓ Step 2: Know Your Blind Spots

What feedback have you resisted but might be true?

✓ Step 3: Choose a Leadership Principle

Pick one of the five core traits to grow this month.

✅ Step 4: Take a Micro-Action

Send a note of encouragement. Ask a teammate for input. Learn something new.

✅ Step 5: Define Your Legacy

What do you want your team to say about you when you're not in the room?

🎙 Final Thoughts: Leadership Is Who You Are Becoming

This isn't about reaching the top of the org chart. This is about leading with courage, compassion, and clarity.

The radio industry is changing. The world is changing. And the leaders who will shape the future are the ones who are flipping the format on fear—one decision, one conversation, one moment at a time.

Now is your moment.

Go be the leader you were meant to be.

CONCLUSION

The Frequency of Fear Has Been Flipped

W.K.R.P. Framework Recap: Your Full-Spectrum Signal for Leadership

Winning Mindset — Know Thyself — Resilience & Responsibility — Positive Psychology

You Made It. But This Isn't the End.

Congratulations. If you've reached this point, you've done more than read a book—you've begun a transformation. From the first chapter to this final page, you've unpacked the mindset traps, leadership myths, emotional baggage, and outdated models that have kept far too many professionals stuck in fear.

You didn't just learn a few tips. You got a full rewire.

Now, let's recap what you uncovered in the twelve chapters of this journey.

W: Winning Mindset

1. *Chapter 1: Why Fear is Running the Show (And How to Flip It)*

2. You explored how fear often dictates decisions in the radio industry—and how awareness, presence, and conscious reframing are the keys to flipping that fear into purpose-driven leadership.

3. *Chapter 2: Understanding the Science of Fear and Failure*

4. You learned about the biological and psychological underpinnings of fear, including how stress responses hijack creativity—and how understanding this can give you back control.

5. *Chapter 3: Reprogramming Your Brain for Confidence and Creativity*

6. With the tools of neuroplasticity, gratitude, and visualization, you began training your brain to stop defaulting to fear—and start aligning with confidence, courage, and clarity.

K: Know Thyself

- Chapter 4: *Own Your Identity: Strengths over Self-Doubt*

- You explored what makes you you — beyond the title, the ratings, or the resume. You named your strengths, acknowledged your values, and realized that leadership is an inside-out process.

- Chapter 5: *The Truth About Confidence*

- In this chapter, you rewired the belief that only the loudest person in the room is the most secure. You learned that quiet confidence, grounded in self-knowledge, is often the most powerful signal of all.

- Chapter 6: *Respect, Teamwork, and Culture Building*

- Culture isn't coffee mugs and slogans—it's the emotional tone of your team. You developed strategies for setting boundaries, fostering trust, and creating a workplace where people want to show up.

R: Resilience, Responsibility & Respect

- Chapter 7: *Building Resilience and Managing Setbacks*
- You acknowledged that failure isn't fatal—it's feedback. You learned how to bounce, adapt, and keep moving through adversity without losing your momentum.
- Chapter 8: *The Power of Responsibility in Leadership*
- Taking responsibility isn't about taking the blame—it's about owning your impact. You stepped into accountability and discovered how it builds trust and strength.
- Chapter 9: *The Art of Resilience in a Changing Industry*
- In radio and in life, the only constant is change. You began to view challenges as opportunities to grow, adapt, and lead with authenticity instead of fear.

P: Positive Psychology

- Chapter 10: *Positive Psychology for Broadcasters*
- You tapped into the science of what works—gratitude, strengths-focus, emotional intelligence, and psychological safety. You discovered how positivity isn't fluff—it's fuel.
- Chapter 11: *The Future of Radio and Adapting to Change*
- You learned how to flip the signal from fear to flow, from panic to presence. You rewired your mindset for creativity, collaboration, and confidence in uncertain times.
- Chapter 12: *Becoming the Leader You Were Meant to Be*
- Leadership isn't about titles—it's about showing up. You defined your values, named your style, and committed to becoming the kind of leader who elevates others.

Mike McVay's Insider Insight; What I've learned - Recap my Comments & Stories.

Winning Mindset: Anything is possible. Everything is on the table. I have great faith in myself in that if I don't know how to do something, I will figure out how to do it. I'm not afraid to admit mistakes and ask for a "Redo." Failure is a part of success. Given that business isn't a game with a final buzzer, it's easy to work past what others may consider failure, and it's on the way to Success.

Know Thyself; What are your strengths and weaknesses. Are the weaknesses something you can strengthen, or are they a trait to be diminished in importance to your career. Are the strengths you have dominant? Can those strengths be applied in a way that makes the team stronger? If your super power is being a good listener, then listen. If it's to motivate others, then do that. If you are an energetic driver, do so, but with caution as not all people are motivated by that fashion of leadership.

Resilience, Responsibility, & Respect; There's no end to this game. If you have a bad rating sweep, a bad weekly, lose a high-profile talent, hit the proverbial "wall." Back-up and find a new direction.

Resilience is a trait that successful leaders have in their blood. Responsibility is what comes with the role of being a leader. It's the weak leader who finds fault with others. A strong leader shows the way back to the path of success.

Respect is earned, not demanded. That's what you will read and hear, over and over in leadership books. While I do believe that it's true, I don't agree that you shouldn't demand respect. Earn the respect of your team by respecting them. Demand respect in a softer way that underscores the expectations you have for them and how they should perform. A favorite saying of one of my mentors was "People respect what you inspect." I believe that's true.

Positive Psychology: I come from the school of thinking that no one awakes in the morning with a plan to sabotage my day. I expect that everyone wants what I want in the way of accomplishing success. A smile, positive energy, a collaborative atmosphere, and having fun. It's tough to be negative when everyone around you is having fun.

You Have the Blueprint

You now have a complete map to flip the format on fear:

- 📷 A mindset rooted in purpose, not panic.
- 💡 Emotional intelligence that enhances creativity and connection.
- 💬 Communication that builds clarity instead of chaos.
- 🚀 Leadership that fuels trust and innovation — regardless of your job title.

Every worksheet, every Victorville story, every Apple A Day entry, every trade insight was designed to help you lead with confidence.

You don't need permission. You don't need to wait. You already have the signal.

Now it's time to transmit it.

Next Steps: Stay Connected & Keep Growing

Download the *Flipping the Format on Fear* App for daily and weekly guidance, FAQs, and encouragement. Inside, you'll find:

1. Daily Apple A Day messages

2. Tips for a Badass Attitude

3. Leadership support and mindset tools

4. Audio insights and worksheets to stay on track

Follow the journey on Substack, YouTube, and Instagram. Join the conversation. Share your story. Tag a mentor.

Get the App and join the program!

Details here:

Cue the Music. Cue the Mic. Cue the Mindset.

Let's keep flipping the format—together.

You are *Licensed2BBadass*. And the airwaves need your voice.

This is only the beginning.